That Compassionate
Touch of
MA ANANDAMAYEE

That Compassionate Touch of
MA ANANDAMAYEE

NARAYAN CHAUDHURI

MOTILAL BANARSIDASS PUBLISHERS
PRIVATE LIMITED • DELHI

First Edition: Delhi, 1980
Reprint: 1986, 1998

ISBN: 81-208-0204-7 (Cloth)
ISBN: 81-208-0210-1 (Paper)

MOTILAL BANARSIDASS

41 U.A. Bungalow Road, Jawahar Nagar, Delhi 110 007
8 Mahalaxmi Chamber, Warden Road, Mumbai 400 026
120 Royapettah High Road, Mylapore, Chennai 600 004
Sanas Plaza, Subhash Nagar, Pune 411 002
16 St. Mark's Road, Bangalore 560 001
8 Camac Street, Calcutta 700 017
Ashok Rajpath, Patna 800 004
Chowk, Varanasi 221 001

PRINTED IN INDIA

BY JAINENDRA PRAKASH JAIN AT SHRI JAINENDRA PRESS,
A-45 NARAINA INDUSTRIAL AREA, PHASE I, NEW DELHI 110 028
AND PUBLISHED BY NARENDRA PRAKASH JAIN FOR
MOTILAL BANARSIDASS PUBLISHERS PRIVATE LIMITED,
BUNGALOW ROAD, DELHI 110 007

FOREWORD

Among all the living Godmen of India or for that matter even Godwomen, Ma Anandamayee "is the most shining diamond in the luminous crown of contemporary Indian spiritual life." Initially known as a strange village girl in what was then East Bengal (now Bangladesh), She grew up to be known as the miraculously compassionate Mata Anandamayee— Mother of Joy. Her acts of love and compassion to those around as well as away from Her have become almost a legend, serving as a perennial source of faith in Her.

Those who have already come in contact with Sri Anandamayee Ma seem never to tire of reading or knowing more and more about Her. This desire is more persistent among those who have merely heard about Her but have not yet had the opportunity of having Her *darshan.* The number of Mother's devotees is vast and ever-growing, and they come from all walks of life and from almost all over the world. Their eagerness to know more about Mother's personality, Her compassion and teachings is growing day by day. It is for the benefit of these devotees that has prompted the author to bring out this volume. It is partly a compilation of miraculous incidents depicting Mother's infinite compassion for Her children and partly a narration of miracle-laden incidents witnessed by the author. It also contains strange little happenings signifying Her divine glories. Besides being the only one of its kind amongst other books published so far about Mother Anandamayee, this book is written by one who has known Her for over three decades and who was the Managing Editor of the prestigious journal *Ananda Varta* which is published from Mata Anandamayee Ashram, Varanasi.

Each incident of this volume unmistakably shows that Mother lives solely for Her fellow-beings and for helping and guiding them to become "pilgrims on the Supreme Path — the Path that leads to Self-realization, to supreme ultimate God Itself." Indeed, She is looked upon as an incarnation of unbounded divine compassion.

Like the spiritual magnates in history, e.g. Lord Buddha, Jagadguru Sri Sankaracarya, Lord Gouranga and others, Ma Anandamayee travels the length and breadth of India spreading the message of love and showing the path to infinite peace and happiness. To quote Mother's words, "Indeed everything that this body says or does — its actions, movements, its going hither and thither — is done for your sakes. Whatever is done for you by this body at any time, it is you who cause it to happen."

It is no doubt an immensely pleasing sight today that from all parts of the globe, men and women, young or old, are gathering near Her to seek solace and peace. Under the magic touch of Mother's unbounded affection and compassion for Her children, a hankering is growing even amongst the agnostics to be "travellers in the Path of Immortality."

Mahamahopadhyaya Pandit Gopinatha Kaviraja has said: "We know very well that in every stage of

Her life, Mother played Her part admirably well consistently with the laws of propriety befitting Her role, and yet behind all these appearances She retains the self-same and eternally self-revealed consciousness. It is, therefore, a very difficult task to try to describe Mother Anandamayee as She really is. She has appeared differently to different persons and even if these differences are contradictory, we can quietly accept them knowing fully well that in a higher synthesis even contradictories may meet together. These differences need not be obliterated in the interest of a particular viewpoint. Naturally we do not, and cannot, know all the phases of Mother's life; and that the little we know of a particular phase, we know imperfectly. She is too near us to be seen in Her proper perspective and as for ourselves, we too shall have to rise up to the height and attain to broad outlook in which an attempt may be made to study Her properly. What is really needed is to feel that She is Mother and we are Her children and that as mere children, we cannot be expected to know Her as She is but only as She shows Herself to us in response to our cravings. It really becomes us to behave as infants crying out in the night and invoking Mother with an inarticulate language for Her actual descent and benediction."

It is hoped that besides being popular with those who have already come in contact with Ma Anandamayee, this book will in general be sought by all those who need an introduction to Her teachings and an inspiration to know more about Her.

Narayan Chaudhuri

ACKNOWLEDGEMENTS

In bringing out this volume, help has been derived from the following publications and for which the author's grateful thanks are due to their publishers:

(1) Ananda Varta Journal
(2) Ma Anandamayee by Devotees (long out of print)

CONTENTS

CONTENTS

Chapter 1

"COME AGAIN"

I

It all happened in the summer of 1941. I had the first *darsan* of Sri Sri Ma Anandamayee in May 1941 at Simla, the summer capital of India. I was then serving in the Defence Department which was at that time functioning from Simla. How we all remember that fateful year 1941 and all the horrors and calamities let loose by the Second World War!

One day, at lunch time, I decided to have a good walk to straighten my limbs and ward off the monotony of endless war-time work. I followed the road which leads to Simla Kalibari, a Kali temple-cum-residential establishment managed and run by the Bengali residents of Simla. As I came near it, I heard some *kirtan* going on inside the temple accompanied by mridang and cymbals. I could distinctly hear the words of the *kirtan* — "Hare Krishna Hare Krishna Krishna Krishna Hare Hare; Hare Rama Hare Rama Rama Rama Hare Hare." It was being sung in a melodious tune. I was seized with the curiosity to know the occasion for the *kirtan,* and with that end in view I went right inside and found that the *kirtan* was being sung and conducted by a band of devotees by going round and round a centrally erected *manch* (altar) inside a well-decorated big hall. For some time I stood entranced with the *kirtan* but could not find anyone near by to enlighten me about the occasion. So I decided to leave, and as I turned back to go, I saw a Brahmachariji approaching me from the other side. I at once seized the opportunity and asked him about the occasion for the *kirtan*. He said, "Ma Anandamayee is here and that is why Astaprahar (a 24-hour non-stop *kirtan*) is going on." I said, "I have heard the name of Mother but I hadn't had the opportunity and good fortune to have her *darsan* so far. Is it by any chance possible to meet her now?" His right hand pointed towards a set of rooms on the other side of the satsang hall and he said, "Ma is in one of those rooms. You may just try your luck." With these words he hurriedly disappeared, leaving me in two minds as to whether it would be right and proper to invade that sanctum sanctorum at that inappropriate hour, which was lunch time for all. After overcoming my hesitation and with a palpitating heart, I had taken only a few steps towards my goal when I found a burly middle-aged lady, apparently a close devotee of Ma, emerged from one of those rooms and moved quickly towards me as if to bar my advance. When she came and stopped before me with a grave air and stern look, my heart seemed to miss a beat. She was wearing a light yellow-coloured dhoti and her hair was cut short. I at once realized that I should not have encroached upon that prohibited area without permission or escort and hence felt apologetic. In a deep voice the lady asked, "What do you want?" I somehow mumbled, "I hear that Ma Anandamayee is here and I hadn't had the good luck so far to have her *darsan*. Is it possible to have her *darsan* now?" The reply came in a more unhelpful and unwelcome tone, "Do you think it is the proper time for *darsan?* It's about half past one now and Ma is having a rest. You may come some other Time."

The reply convinced me that the god of luck was unkind to me. Moreover, the *darsan* of a saint was no easy come-and-go affair. Its pre-requisites are devotion and sadhana none of which I was endowed with. To crown it all, it was utterly wrong on my part to act out of bravado and seek *darsan* at an undisputedly wrong hour. The lady's reply made me shrink within and I didn't hazard any repetition of my request before that august personality. Without any further word, I decided therefore to retreat and proceeded towards the exit. This misadventure disheartened me a lot and I quickened my steps to leave. No sooner had I approached the exit door, than unexpectedly I heard the same lady address me in a softer tone, "Are you really going away?" I stopped and on turning back I found her standing at the same place but now in a relaxed attitude and not so unwelcome mood. But her question was not very clear to me because after her summary dismissal of me with her firm declaration that Mother was taking a rest and that *darsan* at that time was quite impossible, what else could I do but to go away? However, on my coming back to her, the following conversation ensued:

Q.   What do you do here?

Ans.   I work here in the office of the Defence Department of the Govt. of India.

Q.   From where are you coming now?

Ans.   Direct from office. It's now lunch time.
Q.   "I see. Well, wait a minute, let me see."

With these words, she hurried towards the room from which she had emerged. I, on the other hand, stood perplexed wondering at the sudden and unexpected turn of events as well as change in the attitude of my questioner. A faint ray of hope then flashed into my mind at the possibility of fulfilment of my desire to have a darsan of Ma.

But I did not have to wait long, for after a couple of minutes, the same lady beckoned me to her, and as soon as I came near, she whispered, "Go inside, Ma is in. Do obeisance to her and come out at once. Do not attempt to talk to her as it is now her resting time." I nodded to confirm that I would follow her instructions, and without tarrying for fear of being saddled with any further restrictions, I immediately entered the holy room - my journey's end.

I subsequently came to know that the lady who was instrumental in arranging my first *darsan* of Ma at that seemingly wrong hour, was no other person than our revered Didi Gurupriya Devi, who is not only a constant companion of Ma, but also a noble soul who is constantly engaged in serving her. Later on, when I was intimately acquainted with her, I came to know that Didi's exterior is as hard as nails but her interior is softer than flowers.

After gaining entrance into Mother's room in the manner mentioned above, I observed at first only a mass of lustrous brilliance in the sitting posture on a cot, a mass that looked like a human form completely covered with a cloud of whiteness. I express my utter inability to explain in words the impact of that unearthly phenomenon. Was it due to the fact that I had entered Mother's room after remaining quite some time in the blazing sunshine outside and it took some time for my eyes to adjust vision in the semi-darkness inside the room? Or was it a stellar orbit of Divine refulgence that always encircles Ma's Divine Being but remains mostly invisible? I have since heard a few fortunate devotees say that they have seen such a circle of light around her face and head as indeed this halo is always there. I therefore consider myself one of those fortunate few to whom Ma graciously granted a purified vision, a glimpse of her Divine Light. However, after a few moments, Ma's whole feature and her smiling divine face which appeared to me like a flower in full bloom, became clearly visible. I at once realized that Ma in her infinite kindness drew me out for a while from the realm of darkness in order to grant me a glimpse of the World of Light. Does this not testify to Mother's boundless, causeless and unaccountable grace upon her children?

I then did my obeisance to her and remained in a knelt-down position thoroughly oblivious of everything of this world and dazed by the unforgettable vision that I had a few moments ago. I had the least awareness of Didi's stealthy entrance and the way she had positioned hereself just behind me. I came to my normal self at the mild admonition of Didi who hissed, "Make haste. Ma will rest now." Before I obeyed her, I bent my head down on the ground to do obeisance, and as I raised my head, Ma asked, "Do you live here (Simla)?" I replied, "No Mother. The office in which I work is now here. It remains

here during the summer and moves down to New
Delhi in winter." Ma nodded and said, "COME
AGAIN". She then stretched out her right hand and
Didi taking the hint, placed an apple on her hand
and Ma in turn gave it to me. I then did obeisance
once again and came out of the room with my heart
overflowing with joy and divine peace.

I waited a couple of minutes outside Ma's room
for Didi so that I could thank her and express my
gratitude for arranging this unexpected and wonderful *darsan* of Ma. But minutes ticked away and Didi
did not come out. My watch showed that the lunch
time was about to be over and I, therefore, hurried
towards office.

On my way to office, I felt I was possessed with
some wonderful delight and peacefulness to which I
had hitherto been a stranger. My heart seemed to
have been charged with some unearthly current
which had magnetised it and soothed each little fibre
and tissue in it. It was certainly my luckiest day to
have an unexpected *darsan* of Ma and that too at
such an improper time. But one question was uppermost in my mind — how could it all happen and
how was the impossible suddenly turned into reality?
The more I pondered over the sequence of events
leading up to *darsan,* the more I was drawn to the
irresistible conclusion that all that happened at Ma's
will and grace. Because, first, the appearance of
Brahmachariji just at the right moment when I was
about to leave the place, secondly, the presence of
Didiji as if from nowhere, thirdly, her blunt order of
dismissal first and then sudden change of her mind,
her calling me back and ultimately arranging for the

darsan all these were nothing but unmistakable doings of Ma from behind as if she was pulling the strings and directing the course of events through Brahmachariji and Didi who acted as mediums. Call it a miracle or mere coincidence, the very fact of allowing a petty person like me to have an untimely *darsan* and causing it to happen through Her Divine will, is a clear example of Mother's 'ahetuk kripa' (spontaneous grace) and boundless compassion. When I re-entered office and sat at my desk, Ma's last two words "COME AGAIN" continued to ring in my heart.

II

There are in this world a few rare living luminaries who shed divine lustre of grace and compassion all around wherever they happen to be. One can neither forget them even after one chance meeting nor brush away from memory their spoken words. This was exactly the feeling I had after my first *darsan* of Ma. But, strangely enough, although Ma said "Come Again" during my first *darsan,* I could not make it. I could not meet her for the second time during her stay for the next two days in Smila. Perhaps it was not to be as it was not lotted for me. I had second *darsan* of Ma in Delhi after a lapse of three months. But alas, the second *darsan* was quite different and disappointing in comparison with the first. While the first *darsan* filled me with joy, happiness and peace, the second one left me disheartened and despondent.

It happened like this. In those days, when our New Delhi Ashram at Kalkaji was under construction, Ma used to stay in the compound of Dr. J.K.Sen's house at Hanuman Road in a seperate block of rooms built specially for her use. One day, on receiving information about her arrival in Delhi, I went after office hours straight to Dr. Sen's house. Outside the house, a cluster of motor cars assured me of Ma's presence inside. On going near the portion of Ma's block, I noticed that Ma was sitting inside a circular room, obviously built and used for satsang, surrounded by many devotees, the majority of whom were ladies. It looked impossible for me to pierce through that cordon and go near Ma. I therefore took my position behind a group of devotees who were standing at a distance and watching Ma. Ma was then narrating a story obviously to make home a point raised in a question by somebody and everybody was enjoying the story with rapt attention.

Those who have had the opportunity and good fortune of hearing stories from Ma by sitting near her, must have noticed and enjoyed her captivating style and intimate way of story-telling. In order to make a questioner understand an intricate point of sadhana or spiritual practice or experience, Ma would sometimes start telling a story, and during the process, she would very often raise her hands in significant movements, occasionally would strike one palm with the other and at times would burst into scintillating laughter. The effect of all these is magical on listeners who not only remain spell-bound all through but also get a spontaneous feeling of transportation to another world — a world free from sorrows amd unhappiness but full of peace and tranquillity, light and *ananda.* It is a common experience that at the end of such a story, not only the questioners feel amply rewarded, but the listeners present are also gratified with a rare treat.

This in short is the story Ma told:

Somewhere a person died, and it was decided by his friends and relatives to perform the last rites on the bank of the Ganga which was a long way off. It was night time. When the dead body was being carried to the distant cremation ground, a lashing storm attended with torrential rain broke out making further progress impossible. The bier-carriers had no other alternative than to leave the bier with the corpse on the road and run for shelter. On reaching there they fell asleep due to extreme fatigue. Not far from this place there lived a very old and destitute woman whose condition due to prolonged illness was very serious at that time. She had a long-cherished desire to breathe her last on the bank of Ganga, but how it could be possible she knew not. Then in that night of rain and storm, she heard about that dead body left temporarily due to inclement weather. This she thought to be a God-gifted opportunity which she decided to avail of. She somehow went near the forsaken bier, managed to unfasten the dead body and drag it to nearby nallah (drain) full of water. She then took the place of the dead body on the bier, covered herself fully with a cloth and lay still. After sometime when the weather was clear, the carriers of the bier returned and raised the bier on their shoulders without a semblance of suspicion of any foul play in their mind and proceeded towards the cremation ground. On reaching the bank of the Ganga, they started making necessary.arrangements for performing the last rites. In the meanwhile the old woman breathed her last. In this way, her desire was fulfilled as it was destined to be. Ma then ended the story with the following conclusion: "God in His supreme kindness and infinite compassion makes whatever arrangements are necessary for the bestowal of anything that is lotted to each one of us just at the proper time and place." What an excellent conclusion and teaching which, once heard, remains engraved for ever in the listener's heart! The lesson, therefore, that one should draw and abide by is that we will never be deprived of anything that has been allotted to us by God. But alas, what a pity it is that we cannot keep ourselves satisfied with this Divine Promise, as we are by nature prone to take it as uncertain. This leaves us fussing and fretting for the non-achievement of anything that we think we are entitled to have at any self-chosen hour. This reminds us of Gurudev Rabindranath Tagore's immortal words: "What we want, we want in error; what we get we want not."

At the conclusion of the story, Ma got up to leave and the devotees rushed rather unseemly to do obeisance to her. Ultimately a queue was formed, and after standing in the queue for quite some time when my turn came to go near Ma and do pranam, I noticed that Ma looked at me only for a second or two and then turned her eyes away. That fleeting look of hers appeared to me as an empty look devoid of attention or recognition. I, however, did pranam but with a heart full of disappointment and uneasiness. I then moved out of the queue to enable the next man to avail of his turn. My mind was agitated particularly at the painful thought that Ma could not recognize me which I fondly hoped she would do. Of course, she had seen me only once in the past and that too for a short while. Was that brief encounter sufficient for Ma to recognize me after a lapse of three months? Who knows? Afterwards when I thought over this incident in leisure, I reasoned that this happened as I had in the niche of my heart a false vanity and an empty pride that Ma would surely recognise me and speak a few words as she did during the first *darsan.* I derived some consolation from this line of reasoning that Ma's look of non-recognition was purposeful to smash up that baneful vanity for my ultimate good. But I was at a loss to figure out the motive and significance of Ma's words "COME AGAIN" spoken during my first visit. Being unable to get at the underlying meaning of those words, I came to the conclusion that those words had no importance whatsoever; they were words of formality which Ma perhaps tells everybody who visits her for the first time. This conclusion, however, filled me with deep disappointment, as a result of which I lost all interest and inspiration to visit her again.

That I lost inspiration to go to her again was not beyond the knowledge of all-knowing Ma, and I came to realise this fact a month later through an unforgettable dream. In the afternoon of a holiday in Delhi, I dreamt that I was walking along a long lonely road. After going about half a mile, a clear

sound of kirtan entered my ears which was coming
from inside the compound of a Govt. Quarter in
New Delhi. On going near the gate of the quarter, I
found a group of persons doing kirtan under a big
tree. All the kirtanias (singers) appeared to be
Bengalees and this roused my curiosity which prompted me to pass through the gate and stand near the
singers. After enjoying the *kirtan* for some time, I
looked toward the main building and imagine my
great surprise to find no other person but Shree
Shree Anandamayee Ma who stood leaning against
the main door of the front room. When my gaze was
fixed on her, my surprise knew no bounds to notice
that Ma raised her right hand and made a beckoning
sign towards me. I thought she was signalling someone among the singers. But all of them were engaged
and absorbed in *kirtan* and were oblivious of Ma's
presence on the verandah. To make sure that she
wanted me, I touched my breast with a finger and
she readily nodded with approval. On approaching
Ma with quick steps, I did pranam and as I raised my
head and stood up, Ma asked: "Do you want to have
a rosary?" I was non-plussed at Ma's sudden suggestion of offering me a rosary, the desire of having one
never arose in my mind. Moreover, no such desire
ever rose in my mind to request her for a rosary.
Why then, this offer of rosary to me? While Ma was
waiting for an answer, I stood perplexed. After some
time I ventured to say, "Ma, I am already initiated
and my Guru never told me to pray by counting over
the beads of rosary." Ma replied: "That does not
prevent you from accepting a rosary which will help
you do namjapa (repetition of God's name) daily for

a longer time." Ma then turned back without waiting for my answer and led me to a room. She settled herself on a cot and I sat down on a carpet. She then took out a rosary of medium-sized Rudraksha beads from underneath her pillow and placing it in my hands instructed me to turn the rosary with a particular mantra which she uttered to me. I then did pranam and as I raised my head from the ground, I suddenly woke up from my sleep and realised that I was dreaming. The rest of the night was spent in ruminating over what I saw in the dream. I also realized that through the medium of the dream Ma obliterated the pain, anguish and disappointment that had gathered in my mind during the second *darsan* a month back. I was also convinced that in her own supernatural manner, Ma had revived my lost inspiration to go to her again.

It is said the words uttered by saints and Mahatmas do not go unfulfilled, and its reason is that they charge their words with requisite power for their self-fulfilment. They do not seem to depend on ordinary mortals for fruition of whatever words they utter, perhaps for the simple reason that human beings are nothing but mere winding dolls and like them are pathetically helpless and solely dependent on an Invisible Power for every thought, word or deed.

Next time I met Ma at Varanasi Ashram after a fortnight. One day having obtained permission to talk in private with her, I narrated to her the details of the dream I had. She very graciously advised me to see her the next day with a rosary of mediumsized Rudraksa beads. I was lucky to get a good rosary

with the kind help of Swami Sankaranandaji of the
Ashram and showed it to Ma the following day. Ma
took the rosary in her hands, touched every bead of
it and returned it to me with the instruction to turn it
daily with the same mantra I got in dream. In this
way, what happened in dream, turned into reality
and from then on started my "coming again and
again" to Ma through her boundless grace and infinite
compassion. JAI MA.*

---

*Incident of the Author's first *darsan* of Ma.

Chapter 2

"NOW YOU MAY TAKE OVER"

At times some moments come in the lives of all of us when we stand face to face with a situation, phenomenon or incident, the purport of which is not readily comprehensible. But such things in relation to Mother carry one particular message, the message of infinite compassion and some deeper significance that cannot at first be captured by thought. On conclusion of her action, it becomes invariably and universally clear that whatever she does, she does it out of compassion for her devotees.

I remember one such incident which I witnessed at our New Delhi Ashram about 18 years ago. One day, as was usual in the evening, Ma was sitting on a cot in the big hall of the Ashram for giving her devotees *darsan*. As soon as she settled on her seat, everybody present started doing pranam one by one. At the end of it, she composed herself to a stillness which defused a blissfully soothing radiation all around. All of us sat absorbed and engulfed in divine peace in that heavenly atmosphere. It is the common experience of everybody who has ever sat in such an atmosphere with Ma sitting nearby, that he or she feels within what life is like in its boundlessness as opposed to our mundane, woeful and restless life. I had asked several people, particularly Europeans, about how they felt after such sittings. The spontaneous and unanimous answer was that for the time being they felt to have been transported to another world and secondly they seemed to have the supernatural feeling of being bathed by a transcendental Light emanating from the physical being of Ma. Such was also the experience of those who had gathered at the New Delhi ashram on that particular evening.

Minutes ticked by. After about half an hour, Ma nodded to an Ashram girl. As she went near, Ma whispered something to her. Only two words "hot water" came to my ears as I was sitting near by. The girl hurried out of the hall on her errand. Ma next called another Ashram girl who was asked to keep ready two pieces of white cloth rolled like bandages. She also ran on her mission. A third girl was instructed to keep handy two strips of flat wood. These things, as we all know, are essential first-aid items in cases of accidents or injuries. But none apparently among those present seemed to need immediate attention with hot water and bandages or any sort of medical care, nor any Ashramite was heard to be afflicted with any accident or injury. Why then this hurry to keep the first-aid items in readiness? We all were highly intrigued.

The mystery was uncovered shortly afterwards. After about ten minutes, a murmuring noise was heard outside, and almost immediately an elderly woman, groaning with pain, was carried in the arms of four persons inside the hall. As soon as she was lowered slowly on the floor in the middle of the hall, Ma came hurriedly to her and asked in a soothing voice: "What has happened, Ma?" The lady, though in much pain, raised her both hands slowly, folded them in the posture of doing pranam and stammered: "Ma, I met with an accident on the way while coming to you. My right knee seems to have been broken."

The details of the accident came from her companions who said: "The lady started in her car from her house at Pusa Road, New Delhi, with the intention of coming to Kalkaji Ashram for a *Darsan* of Ma. While negotiating a sharp bend near Kailash Colony, which is about three miles off from the Ashram, a truck bumped into the car, giving it a tremendous jolt. As a result, the driver of the car was thrown out while the lady fell down from her seat and her right knee struck heavily against the back side of the front seat the impact of which had possibly fractured her knee. As she was in a terrible pain, the owner of a car which stopped just then near the place of accident, offered immediately to carry her to a hospital. But surprisingly the lady refused to be taken to a hospital and implored instead to transport her to Mataji's Ashram. She was heard repeating that however serious the nature of injuries might be and how much she might suffer due to resulting pain from her disabled knee, she must be taken to Mataji first as she had started from her house with that resolve and it did not matter what happens to her afterwards. She was therefore brought to the Ashram on her insistence. Ma heard the details of the accident looking all the time at the patient who now seemed to be happy due perhaps to the thought of having the rare good luck of lying so long at Ma's feet which everybody like her considers to be a far safer and surer resort for cure than a hospital.

Ma then signalled the Ashram girls to bring in the first-aid materials which she had advised earlier to keep handy. The onlookers of this drama were now amazed to uncover the mystery of keeping hot water and bandages ready and to have a glimpse of Ma's supernatural power of knowing and foreseeing an incident happening or about to happen at a distant place. The purpose of keeping first-aid items ready was then clear to all and it was equally clear that while the lady was meeting with an accident far away from the Ashram, Ma, though seated in the Ashram hall, was seeing every bit of it. She was not only seeing what was happening to one of her devotees at a distance, but she also could know beforehand that the injured lady would be brought to the Ashram soon and that is why she wanted to keep everything ready to meet the emergency.

The girls then began to attend to the patient. They started fomenting the injured knee with cotton dipped in hot water under Ma's careful vigil. After about ten minutes of fomentation, the injured part was bandaged, under Ma's expert guidance and advice, with two pieces of wood-sheets, cotton and bandages. On Ma's suggestion, a girl then brought a glass of hot milk mixed with pure ghee and placed the glass in Ma's hand. Ma held the glass for a minute or so, looked at its content and then returned it to the girl. With Ma's instruction, the girl sat by the side of the patient, raised her head with one hand and supporting it with her body, raised the glass with her other hand to the mouth of the lady to enable her drink the milk slowly. The whole operation was conducted and executed with care and precision under Ma's merciful direction.

Ma then returned to her seat, and as there was no doctor available at that time in the Ashram, she asked somebody to call for one. The doctor arrived after half an hour. Ma gave him the details of the accident and mentioning what she had done by way of first-aid application, said: "Pitaji, I have done whatever little known to a novice like me. Now you may take over." The doctor replied: "Ma, you have done everything considered essential in such cases leaving very little for me to do. With your unfailing magical touch, she will be all right soon. I envy her for her firm faith and devotion to you which made her remember you first as a divine doctor for cure of her fractured knee rather than depend on a petty doctor or hospital."

I came to know afterwards that the lady got completely cured of her knee-fracture and was quite all right through infinite compassion of Ma. Jai Ma.*

Words of Ma

In the first stage to sit for meditation causes uneasiness or pain in one's limbs. When small children start to learn reading they cannot concentrate. How many books they destroy how many they tear to pieces and throw away. They do not understand their value. But slowly and gradually, as they acquire fluency in reading, it gives them joy. At first people

*An incident witnessed by the Author.

study in the hope of becoming rich, but later
they come to understand the value of knowledge. By labouring hard, practice is acquired.
With how much zeal do you learn in order to
pass your examinations. Finally you become
B.A's and M.A's. But here we are concerned
with Supreme Knowledge (Brahmavidya). At
first the mind does not become steady and
one cannot find any delight in the repetition
in the Name of God or in meditation. The
mind is concerned with bodily comforts, just
as children spoil their books. By Japa, meditation or other spiritual exercises, one's thinking
has to be brought under control. By practice,
the mind becomes steady.

Chapter 3

GLIMPSES OF MOTHER'S DIVINE
COMPASSION

Lila One

It was Easter 1942. I had gone to meet Mataji in the Kishenpur Ashram on the Dehradun-Mussoorie Road. This was my first visit to Ma after I had met her at Lucknow a few months ago. On reaching Dehradun I came to know that some devotees were expected to come from Delhi for their annual kirtan in Mataji's presence. It was to take place on Easter Sunday from sunrise to sunset. On the previous evening, all arrangements were completed. Some of the Dehradun devotees wanted to give a feast (bhandara) on the occasion and sought Ma's permission. She asked, "How many people are you going to provide for?" One of the devotees said, "Two hundred." Mataji remained silent. Another said, "Ma, if you permit, we can make arrangements for, say, three hundred." Still she kept quiet. A third one said, "Ma, without your permission nothing can be done." She looked up and said, "All right, let us hope that your wishes are fulfilled." The market was about five miles away from the Ashram. Provisions had to be obtained at the earliest. The bhaktas were busy.

Next morning the *kirtan* started with due solemnity. The hall and the verandas were all packed, the crowd even overflowing into the garden. Besides listening to the kirtan, everyone wanted to have a glimpse of Ma. The beggars and the sweepers of the locality also turned up. Even passers-by on their way to Mussoorie and other curious sight-seers and tourists, on noticing a crowd, flocked into the Ashram.

At about noon Mataji withdrew from the hall and retired to her small room upstairs. Then she summoned those who were arranging the feast and asked them if they were ready. One of them said frankly, "Mataji, our arrangements are complete, but we had only about four hundred people in view. Now we find that more than five hundred are to be fed." Another: "The market is far off, otherwise something could be done." A third one pleaded, "If we put off the meal until a little later, we might manage." Mataji could no longer remain silent. "It is already noon; are they all not hungry?" She said. After remaining quiet for a while, she added: "No, they are to be fed and fed immediately." Again she stopped for a moment and then spoke with a clear voice: "Make arrangements for serving them now. The meal should be over within an hour and a half. Not one should go away without food. Leave this body alone. Report only if there be any shortage. Otherwise, do not come to me." I was present there. We all felt uncomfortable. But Mataji said with perfect composure, "Go and do as you are told. Do not forget, none should go unfed. Don't be unhappy. God's service must be done with a cheerful heart."

I was perplexed. I was only an onlooker and could not help in any way. I made up my mind, however, to avoid the meal. I no.longer felt hungry. But after a few minutes, Gurupriya Didi came to me in haste, saying, "Dada, please come soon. Haven't you heard Ma's command? Everything must be over in an hour and a half. Won't you help by joining us without delay?" I cast my thoughts aside. Mother had offered the boon of this meal and as her child, I must enjoy it.

I took my seat with the crowd and began to eat the delicious things provided. Everyone was happy. Those who served seemed quite free from anxiety. I ate almost double the usual quantity. The meal proceeded in the midst of a good deal of laughter and merriment with occasional shouts of "Jai Ma".

After the repast, I went upstairs but did not want Mataji to discover me. I stood behind the door of her room and then with a heart filled with serene happiness prostrated, whispering to myself all the while, "Ma, bless me that I may be worthy of a feast like this which brings your grace."

Those in charge of the bhandara were coming up to report to Mataji, since the stipulated hour-and-a-half was over. They opened the door and I found Mataji sitting in her usual tranquil mood. She smiled and asked, "What news?" The devotees cheerfully replied, "Ma, everyone has been fed sumptuously. We never had so much pleasure in serving food." Mataji asked, "What about your provisions?" One of them burst out, "More than five hundred people have eaten and yet there is enough left for two hundred more." Mataji said gravely, "This is very good. Not a particle should be wasted. Let those who come or are staying here be fed again in the evening. Everything must be consumed today. If it cannot be eaten here, let it be given to those outside who are hungry."

We all let her relax for an hour or so. Our minds were busy with the laws of arithmetic: how could eatables for four hundred people satisfy more than five hundred and yet enough be left over for two hundred more? It was indescribably baffling indeed.

Lila Two

Shall I relate another incident of the same afternoon, when five sadhus arrived from Hardwar? There, at a religious meeting, a heated controversy had arisen between them over some passage of the scriptures, for they were of different schools of thought. It was about to end in bitterness when some gentlemen implored them to accept arbitration. It was somewhat difficult to find a suitable arbiter who would be acceptable for purposes of settling the disputed points of the Sastras, particularly to sadhus belonging to different sects. At last they suddenly agreed to refer the matter to Sri Anandamayi Ma. So they had come to her. They entered the Ashram scowling and full of gloom. When they were taken upstairs to Mataji's room, I followed them. Briefly apprised of the situation, Mataji smiled and entreated them to be seated 'in their daughter's room'. Then she asked for fruits and sweets to be brought for their refreshment, but they refused to eat. Mataji insisted, saying, "When you have come to your little daughter, you will have to pay heed to her wishes." This was not a mere request but a command of love.

The sadhus could refuse no longer. Then they asked to be left alone with Ma. After an hour, the door was opened. They came out full of smiles, almost embracing one another. And Mataji's laughter filled the room. I could not help wondering how Ma, untutored in the Sastras, could have settled the dispute.

Lila Three

In 1942, Mataji spent part of the summer in Bhimtal and I was privileged to stay with her. She was repeatedly entreated to visit some ardent devotees in the neighbourhood. She was to return in three or four days, but actually stayed away for eight or ten days. Four or five of us remained at Bhimtal. The weather suddenly changed; there were showers and it grew cold. With Mother away, there was no warmth left in our hearts. My old trouble, asthma, reappeared. I had great difficulty in breathing during the night. Incessant coughing forced me to sit up. I thought of Mataji. When would she come? Just before leaving, she had told me: "Baba, stay here like a good boy." Since I had not been a good boy, I was visited with this malady. How long could I wait without treatment? I wanted to see a doctor in Lucknow, but of course with Ma's permission. But she didn't come.

At last she appeared one evening at dusk. Someone who had accompanied her came running to my room and said, "Dada, how are you? Ma was very anxious to return on your account. For the last few days, she had been repeatedly saying that you were not well. Are you not well? Mataji has come. You will soon be all right." I was no doubt relieved by her return but did not show satisfaction as I was inwardly

displeased and unhappy. When she knew of my
illness, why did she not come earlier?

The person who came to me to report about Ma's
return, went back to her perhaps to inform her about
me. On her way she paused for a moment at the
door of my room and looking towards me said: "Baba,
are you oppressed with trouble? Don't you worry.
Everything will be all right." Then she went away.
Her talk fell flat on me and I found no solace. I now
had to make up my mind to return to Lucknow next
morning for treatment. I did not go to Ma. People
flocked to her room and I could hear them laugh
and rejoice. Perhaps she was relating some of her
experiences. But I was in no mood for such anecdotes. The night was fast approaching. My mind
was overcast with the thought of the troubles and
vexations in store for me during the night. Everyone
there was so happy with the sole exception of my
poor self. Whether I ate anything that evening I do
not remember. But being solitary, brooding and
cheerless, I was feeling that Mataji was cruel, indeed
very cruel, to me. I tried to console myself with the
thought that what was to happen must happen and
that there was no help. I reflected bitterly : "What
am I to Ma?" Such considerations tormented me
and made me even more miserable.

It was past midnight. The paroxysms of asthma,
the difficulty in breathing and the strain of sitting up
for a long time with practically no food, were more
than I could endure silently. I came out of my room
to go to Mataji. The door of her room was ajar. A
lamp was burning inside. Mataji could not possibly
have seen me as I stopped just benind the door. I

hesitated to enter and thought of returning. I then heard Ma's voice, "Come in." My burden was already considerably lightened. I went inside. She said, "Baba, you are suffering much, aren't you?" "I do", I answered, "I am unable to lie down and sleep."

"You will be all right, if you can just lie down and go to sleep", replied Mataji.

"But this is not possible. I have not slept for several nights and I am unable to stand it any longer."

Said Ma after a slight pause, "Do you keep a lamp burning in your room?" "I don't," I replied.

"Do you keep the doors and windows open?"

"Now, I keep one window open for ventilation."

"Do you use a blanket or a quilt?"

"A blanket". I replied.

"That is all right." She was silent for a moment. I also waited. Then she said, "Will you do one thing?"

"I will, Ma, what is it?"

"Close your doors and windows as usual. Put out your lamp and then go to bed. Before lying down, make a clear resolve that you, are going to sleep. And then lie down for rest. Will you do this?" I looked dully towards the wall and said, "I have done all these many times with no effect."

She said with some warmth, "Do it once again as you are now told and do not worry."

I did not know what to say and I kept quiet; then I slowly left the room. I remembered her advice: "Do not worry!" But my mind was occupied. How will it be possible? If I love Ma, it may be possible. If I fix my attention on her, it may be easy. Love alone can calm down all mental disturbances. Thoughts like these continued to ruffle up my mind. I went to my

room. I did as I had been ordered. Before lying
down, I sat on my bed with folded hands in order to
say my prayers but I could not pray. All my pent-up
feelings broke out into sobs and I burst into tears. I
needed rest. Would the divine Mother grant me what
I ·eeded?

I lay down. Within a minute or so my eyes closed
and I fell asleep without any effort. Next morning I
got up late. When I opened the door of my room,
Lina, a sweet little girl-visitor, who is no more alive,
came running and said, "Dada, were you sleeping?
Mataji inquired about you several times." I felt
ashamed of myself and went straight to Mother's
room.

She smiled and said, "Well, Baba, did you get
sleep?"

"I have never had such a sound sleep in my life
before. I felt I was sleeping in the lap of the
MOTHER."

"Yes, it is the MOTHER'S lap where everyone
sleeps. She is loving. Is not sleep a manifestation of
MOTHER?"

That evening, I joined the happy congregation in
Ma's room, laughed and jested with them. But all of
a sudden, I remembered that the night was approaching and feared my trouble might recur. Mataji could
read my thoughts. She at once said, "Baba, do as you
did last night. Just as you did. But you should go to
bed earlier to-night. Better go now and relax." I
prostrated, inwardly praying for her blessing, and
retired. I had plenty of sleep that night as well and
had almost become normal. The third night again

Mataji's counsel bore fruit and I no more feared the recurrence of my troubles.

Next morning I went to Ma when she was alone and said, "It seems to me that I have been cured. There is no trouble now. But do please tell me how you have cured me! You did not give me any medicine, you did neither touch me. When you had looked at me, I could hardly look you in the face, so full of worries and anxieties was I. When you talked, I examined myself and found that I was not worthy of being your son. Tell me, Ma, how have you cured me? Or tell me what to do if the disease recurs." Mataji looked at me with great concern, saying, "Why should the disease recur? It is already gone." I said, "Shall I take it that you have cured me?" Mataji looked up with a smile and said, "You should know that you have cured yourself."

I exclaimed in surprise, "What!"

Mataji repeated with great affection, "It is you who have cured yourself."

I could not understand, but there was no mistaking her love and compassion. I wanted no more. Some of my more sceptical friends ask me at intervals, "Did you have any more attacks?" I am happy to be able to answer them all in the negative. Jai Ma.

Lila Four

One more episode of a still more intimate nature. A son's relation with his mother must always be somewhat personal. But the feeling of love and gratitude or of repentance impels me to put on record some of my experiences so that others may also share them.

It all happened in summer 1943. I had gone to the Ashram in Raipur, Dehradun, for a short respite. On arrival, I came to know that Mataji had also come down from Almora in connection with some yajna (sacrificial ceremony) at Sahasradhara (about five miles from Raipur) and was staying there. I felt happy and eventually met her there the same day. I found her in her usual tranquil mood, shedding happiness all around her. Two or three days later, when the actual rites and ceremonies were over, she came to the Raipur Ashram for a halt. She was to return to Almora very soon. I was a mere witness to the daily gathering of men and women who came from Dehradun and attended on her. I had so far no opportunity to meet her in private. When at last I did so, she said to me, "You are also going to Almora." "Mataji," I replied, "I have not brought the necessary outfit and Almora is a cold place."

"It does not matter, you will be given all you need." I was at the point of arguing but Mataji said: "It is settled then that you are going to Almora."

I remember the state of revolt I was in at that time. I was a prey to the blackest despair. I knew I was helpless and yet resented the idea of being helped. I wanted to be left alone. That was why I had chosen to come to Raipur, a comparatively solitary place, in order to regain the composure of my mind, but Mataji took the task into her hands. I had to accompany her.

We were a party of four including Mataji. The story of our journey from Dehradun to Kathgodam alone would fill pages. But I must hasten to that part of the story which concerns us here. Just before we reached Kathgodam, Mataji disclosed her intention of going to Nainital. This is just like Mataji. She never announces beforehand what she is going to do. I was perplexed. "I am not going," I said. "What is the matter with you?", said Ma. "Nainital is a very cold place, colder than Almora, and you know I have no warm clothes with me."

Mataji interrupted me: "That is known. You will get all you need. So come along. Our stay in Nainital will be very short, say, three or four days, then you will also proceed to Nainital." I had no inclination to go to Nainital, so I looked round and said, "Mataji, you have got so much luggage with you. Allow me to go ahead to Almora and take the extra luggage with me. Those are things meant for the Ashramites of Almora. Why carry them unnecessarily to Nainital?" Mataji seemed to consider my suggestion and then said, "All right, if you want to go, then it cannot be helped."

It was midday. Kathgodam was hot and stuffy. Some lemonade was prepared and given to us. Fruit was also served. Mataji took pains to explain to me all about the road from Almora Motor-Station to the Ashram. It was two miles off. But she told me not to take the undulating bridle path although it was a shortcut. According to her, the motor road was always to be preferred considering my age and strength. I was not paying much heed to these details, as I thought these were known to me owing to my long stay as a teacher at Almora twenty years ago. Yet I was not altogether inattentive, because whatever Mataji says, howsoever light her words, commands attention, partly because of her charming

manner. She then gave me her hurricane lantern
and instructed me to be very careful on my way. I
thought this was but the outcome of a mother's
anxiety for her child. I remember boarding the mail-
car and Mataji standing there watching it go. I felt
proud of the occasion.

As soon as the car began to move, I felt very
unhappy and forlorn. Why did I choose to leave
Ma? The car was ascending the road and the land-
scape should have attracted me. But everything
appeared so humdrum and hackneyed to me. Why
did I not go with Mataji? There was none to talk to
me. I was sitting beside the driver and thinking of
Mataji. Sometimes I would doze off. In this manner,
the tedious journey at last came to an end.

It was dark when I alighted at Almora Station. I
remembered Mataji had given me a lantern. How
very considerate she indeed was! She had anticipated
its need although I had no idea then. The coolies
picked up the luggage and began to move off. I had
given them positive instructions of the route as Mataji
had told me. But they chose the short-cut. I discovered it too late. It was no longer possible to retrace my
steps. So, with some apprehension, I followed them
with unsteady steps. The path became narrow, craggy
and full of sudden ups and downs. I would survey a
few feet of ground with the lantern and then plod
on. My nervousness increased and I almost seemed
to lose my grip over myself. We had then almost
reached the Ashram when my foot slipped; I
stumbled and fell down. One of the coolies threw off
his load and came running. My hands were bruised
and my thighs bled. I had also received a severe jerk

in my hip. Nevertheless I stood up and began to reprimand the coolies. But was it their fault? Like good brothers, they took me to the Ashram where I lay down as I had reached my journey's end.

When Mataji arrived three days later. I was somewhat better, but still confined to bed. The inmates of the Ashram had given me blankets and everything I needed. They were extremely attentive to me and I should have been happy. But the one question that continued always to vex and torment me was: if Mataji had known beforehand of the impending accident, why had she not told me about it?

When Mataji came, I looked eagerly forward to winning her sympathy. So, on her approach, I said, "Ma, I had an accident." But to my mortification I found her stiff. She said, "I do not want to hear." Then she moved in another direction to attend to some sadhus who had come with her from Nainital. It was a sharp rebuff.

Two or three days later, when the sadhus had left for Badrinath and the Ashram had become comparatively quiet, Mataji came to me and said: "Now, what about the accident you had?" I said, "Mataji, the other day I wanted to tell you but you did not want to hear. Today you wish to know, but I do not feel like speaking." Mataji said: "It was for getting this reply from you that the question was asked."

I could no longer endure my condition. I said, "You knew of the accident beforehand but never said a word about it. Instead, you gave me instructions to be followed." Mataji was listening. I continued: "If you think that I am grown up enough to

follow your commandments, I must make it clear
that I do not feel worthy or competent enough to
receive your advice and follow it. I think I am yet an
undeveloped child in that respect. If you can accompany your child in all his troubles and ordeals, I remain
with you. If not, let us part company. The child is
sure to perish. Who can enable a motherless child to
survive?"

I do not know why I spoke in this strain. It was not
a very childlike statement. But I had no time to
analyse myself — perhaps I was incapable of it.
Mataji looked blank like a white sheet of paper. The
next moment there was a great change in her face. I
could discern there all my faults writ large. She had
taken upon herself the burden of my heart. I knelt
down at her feet and my tears showed that I could
no longer think of separation. Jai Ma.

Lila Five

One last episode. This time an episode born of
pure imagination, a dream. Dreams about Mataji
can be narrated by many of us. Mine is a gift to those
who are dreamers like myself. I dreamt I was strolling
through a rural lane. The path moved in a zig-zag
manner, and beautiful flowers and green creepers
were visible on both sides of the fences. There were
gardens and villas on either side. Occasionally there
would be an isolated cottage. I reached a cottage
that was visible from the lane. I slowed down my
pace and stood at the garden-gate and observed
that Mataji could be seen on the verandah of the
cottage. When I saw her, I entered the gate and
seemed to have reached my destination.

When I approached Mataji, I was startled to find that she had a baby on her lap. What was this? There was no one else whom I could ask. I looked at Mataji. She glanced at me but immediately was all attention to the child. How was the infant related to Ma? What an odd question to ask! Are we not all her children? But the question persisted in my mind. I was, no doubt, her son but in what sense was the baby hers? What did it matter if he happened to be the physical son of Mother? So I argued in my dream. Mataji was, all the time, fondling the baby. I thought to myself to put the question in a suitable form. "How does the baby get his nourishment," I asked. Mataji smiled, "Baby does not like milk from outside, I have to suckle him." I felt compassion for Mataji and I began to scrutinize her appearance. She looked considerably reduced and her collar bones were visible. Surely the child was a demon who was sucking her blood and living on it. I began to detest the child. The baby, too, detested me perhaps. Lying on Mataji's lap, he began to stamp his foot on the ground. Was he not kicking at me? So I thought.

Suddenly my feelings changed in my dream. He was, after all, Mataji's own son. If I could love her so much, could I not love her child as well? I looked at the child and tried to feel love for him. Mataji saw my affectionate looks and said, "Would you like to take the baby on your lap?" Realizing that Mataji might get some relief, I at once sat down and extended my arms. Mataji placed the child on my lap. I felt delighted. I began to ask myself, how could I atone for my earlier resentment towards the baby? I had thought of him as a demon. I thought that he wanted to kick me. So if I love him, I must touch him affectionately. I thus touched his right foot and in the inmost depths of my heart tried to feel that I really loved him. But now something occurred that can happen only in a dream. His foot dropped out as if it were an artificial one and alongwith it the entire leg came out, stuck to my hand and dragged my hand towards my own right leg. There the child's limb vanished. I was extremely upset. I quickly placed my fingers on the baby's left foot. The same thing happened: the left foot merged into my own in a similar manner. His right arm and then left, and afterwards all other parts of his tiny body which I was quick in grapsing one after another thinking of them to be separate tangible entities, proved deceptive in the same way, and so the wee form merged into my body, limb by limb, one part after another.

Mataji was looking at me and gauging my quick movements and my growing bewilderment. I also fixed my gaze on her, saying, "Mataji, What is this? This baby, your own baby, is it my own self? Am I this child who looks so ugly and is fond of kicking others and always sucking your life-blood out of you? Do tell me, is it myself? Mataji, do tell me please."

I looked staggered. My whole body was pulsating with excitement. Mataji laughed in her own sweet way. Her peals of laughter were so thrilling and prolonged that they entered into the very marrow of my being. My anxious state, my petty self, in short, my startling dream, all disappeared in the twinkling of an eye.

I was wide awake. It was almost morning. But though no more sleeping, I could still hear Ma's laughter ringing in my ears as if echoing through my room, ultimately finding its way to the world abroad, to mingle with the horizon. It was Mataji who transcended my all and yet left me full. One chapter of my dream-life was over. Jai Ma.

Lila Six

To conclude. Spring 1945. Vasanti Puja[1] was being celebrated in the Banaras Ashram in Mataji's presence. I had also gone there. I passed through the court-yard where people had assembled in groups. I listened to their conversation. Someone was saying: "If Mataji could appear in the form of Sri Krishna, I would accept her without hesitation. You see, I regard Sri Krishna as the complete manifestation of God." I could not hold my tongue. "Brother", I said, "Would you be able to recognize Sri Krishna if he appeared before you in a physical form? Have you ever seen Him?" The man did not retort but he looked extremely discomfited and disturbed. I also fretted and fumed but preferred to move off.

I went upstairs where Mataji was walking up and down the verandah overlooking a part of the Ganges. Some men and women were watching her from a distance. I forgot myself. I reached her and wanted to walk a few steps with her.

But I could not walk without talking. I said, "Mataji, why do I like to speak of you so often and so vehemently and bluntly?" Mataji was listening. I continued, "When I am garrulous, I feel puffed up

---

1. Worship of the goddess Durga in Spring.

with pride. When words fail, depression sets in. I suffer both ways. What shall I do?" Mataji said, "What do you want me to do?" I replied, "Mataji, grant me one favour: make me speechless about you. I think I should not speak of you. All my prattle is an insult to you. It is already oppressing me." I felt relieved when I laid bare my troubled heart before her. It was now her turn to speak. The idol of all adoring hearts, at last opened her lips: "Recognizing me as your daughter, you may say what you think. No harm will touch you. Do you understand?"

I know her to be my mother and myself, her son. Out of this devotion some day, the real spirit of service may be vouchsafed to me. And then the relationship would be reversed: she would become the daughter and I, as she usually calls me, the father. I am waiting for that day of service to dawn in my life.

"They also serve who stand and wait." Jai Ma*

Words of Ma

How much karma (deed) from former births remain yet to be worked out! Just as when, for example, someone has ruined his digestion by indulging in excessive and unrestrained eating; even though he later adopts a frugal and well-regulated diet, the results of these wise measures will not be noticeable straightaway. Thus, whatever be the nature of one's actions at the time, one also has simultaneously to enjoy and suffer the accum-

---

* As narrated by Sri A.P. Banerjee in 'Ma Anandamayee' by devotees which is long out of print.

ulated consequences of one's previous conduct. In God's creation, there is perfect justice. Generally speaking, man is born into this world in order to reap the pleasant results of his good deeds as well as the outcome of his wrong-doing. What about the consequences of any impropriety or injustice he commits at the present time? He will of course have to endure them. Man enjoys the fruits of his accumulated former good works, but he will also have to suffer the effects of his evil deeds. The Almighty's Will is being fulfilled. Man must foster the desire to perform right actions, yet even the impossible becomes possible by God's Will. Let his Lotus-feet be your sole refuge!

While one is guided by reasons, there is always the possibility of straying from the right course. So long as one has not realized that He and He alone is manifest in all modes of being, in all forms, and in the formless, single-mindedness and unswerving faith are indispensable. Such one-pointed devotion must have, for sole aim, the revelation of the Beloved. Living among your people in a spirit of service will be helpful to everybody.

Throughout the twenty four hours, abide in the awareness of the Presence of God. Then only can there be hope of Realization. Who can foresee at what moment He may choose to reveal Himself? This is why one must ever keep wide awake.

Chapter 4

STRANGE LITTLE INCIDENTS DEPICTING MOTHER'S DIVINE GLORIES

One

The Narmada river in Gujarat is said to be the place where practically every stone has the shape of a linga. It is therefore customary to procure Siva-lingas from there. While Mataji was in Vrindaban in December 1964, three lingas were brought from the Narmada for the Rajgir Temple. However, the pandits of Vrindaban for some reason did not approve of those lingas. When Mataji inquired what to do with them, the pandits said they should be put into the Ganga. Since the Ganga is not anywhere near Vrindaban, someone suggested that the Jamuna river could serve the purpose. The day on which the lingas were let down into the river, Mataji felt extremely cold; in fact, She felt so stiff that She could not get up and had the sensation as if Siva was being drowned. She then sent for the pandits and asked them to locate those lingas and have them taken out of the water. The pandits succeeded and Mataji's shivering ceased. The lingas were subsequently sent to Varanasi and later to Rajgir. Mataji remarked that there was a natural connection between Siva and the Ganga. The three lingas in question, however, had

by their immersion in the Jamuna carried the love of
.Krishna to Rajgir

Two
(As narrated by Gauridasi)

One evening in the Ashram at Agarpara, I happened to be sitting quite close to Mataji during Satsang.
Though I was as near to Her as one could be and
directly in front of Her, I could not see Her face. She
was lying down and had Her arms folded and slightly
raised so that Her face was entirely hidden from us.
Like all who have been 'caught' by Her, I had only
one desire which will no doubt sound very foolish to
those who have not been so captivated an intense
longing just to sit there and look upon Her exalted
expression, to see Her eyes that ever seem to be
gazing into the beauty of Eternity. And it appeared
that She was deliberately making that impossible.
Then it occurred to me, this is exactly how God
hides from us in His universe; with the limbs of His
own body, He remains veiled to our sight. I did not
take my eyes off Mataji; neither did I observe Her
move Her arm or raise Her head. *Nevertheless, as
soon as that thought had crossed my mind, I was
suddenly looking straight into Ma's eyes and She
into mine, that still, blissful gaze enveloping me — as
if to say, "At last you have understood a little
something."*

Three

Vrindaban, March 1965. A strange little incident
happened during Mataji's sojourn at Vrindaban. A
Parsi gentleman, who had come for Ma's darshan
from Poona, distinctly noticed that the eyes of the

sculpture of Sri Gauranga in the Nitai-Gauranga temple of our Ashram were moving. *It was exactly like the blinking of a living person. He was nonplussed and went to the temple again the next day. He again found this time only one eye moving perceptively.* He approached the priest and said to him rather sharply: "Why do you use mechanical devices to produce this kind of sensational effect?" The priest could not understand why he was being rebuked and assured him that no device whatsoever was responsible for what he had witnessed. Greatly amazed, the Parsi gentleman reported the matter to Mataji who made him repeat it in Sri Haribabaji's presence. He was told to regard it as a special grace of Lord Gauranga who had given him darshan in this unusual way.

Four

On 31st March 1965, Mataji left New Delhi Ashram for Hardwar where She stayed at Baghat House. There was a severe rainstorm at Hardwar and the daughter of a devotee from Bombay who had accompanied Ma from Delhi, got a severe attack of asthma. The anxious mother wanted to take the child to Delhi by taxi and catch the next plane to Bombay. But Mataji dissuaded her from travelling until the weather cleared up. She then sent a Brahmachari to call a doctor. In that inclement weather, the Brahmachari had no idea how and where to find a good doctor and he was about to inquire. As he stepped out of the gate, a gentleman entered and asked: "Do you think I can have Mataji's darshan at this untimely hour?" (It was about 2 p.m.). "Yes", was the reply from the Brahmachari, "if you are a doctor, you can at once." The gentleman happened to be Doctor Maj. Gen. Sharma from Delhi. He took up the case and the child was all right the next day.

Five

Just as a physician does not concern himself with ascertaining whether his patients are rich or poor, intelligent or stupid, handsome or ugly, good or bad, but treats them simply as ailing men and women whom he has to cure, in a similar way Mataji sees in all human beings her friends. And She meets them accordingly, with friendliness. Here probably lies the secret of her irresistible charm. She never has to exert Herself in order to be friendly or to act in a friendly manner.

In Raipur Ashram, one of the Ashram girls had, it seemed, repeatedly done what the others considered wrong. "Reprimand her", begged the other girls, "she does not listen to us. Do please scold her." Mataji summoned the culprit. The expression on Mataji's face was moving and puzzling at the same time. She obviously tried hard to look severe. But the mask of anger was only too transparent and brittle and Her voice expressed the same play of hide-and-seek behind Her pretended unfriendliness. Suddenly She turned round on Her heel and started laughing heartily. Still laughing, She stood before the girl like a child that has been caught. Ma then said, "Don't you know that I cannot be angry with anyone? How then could I scold her?"

Six

Varanasi, August 1949. Mataji was seated in Her usual place in the hall with only a few ashramites on either side of Her. Nobody had ventured out into the pouring rain. Exactly opposite to Mataji, at the West-end of the hall an emaciated old lady was lying on her bed-clothes that had been spread on the floor. She was very ill and had shifted to the Ashram a few weeks ago, as she wished to die in Mataji s presence and in sight of the Ganga. Her last hour had obviously come. Her son had been called and he was sitting close by her, chanting holy texts, while her daughter was attending on her. The dying woman had a rosary in her hand. She was hardly breathing, though evidently fully conscious. Mataji was watching her intently. Off and on She would shout loudly, "Mother, are you doing japa?" The old lady could respond only through almost imperceptible gestures. Her daughter confirmed, "Yes, Ma, she was doing japa and listening to her son's chanting." Mataji suggested sprinkling Ganga water on her chest, and a few drops of the sacred liquid were instilled into her mouth with a piece of cottonwool as she was too weak to drink. Not for a moment did Mataji let Her eyes off her. Suddenly Mataji got up and walked straight to the dying woman. With great motherly affection, She gazed at her, placed a garland on her chest and then with a swift and determined gesture passed both her hands over the shrivelled body from head to foot. Then the end came. It was an unforgettable and most impressive moment. Blessed are those who end their days in this manner and in the holy presence of Ma.

Seven

In October 1954, the new Ashram at Ranchi was opened in Mataji's presence during the celebration of Durga Puja under a pandal in the open space adjoining the Ashram. At that time it was suggested that an image of Goddess Kali should be installed in the new Ashram. A devotee denoted Rs.1000/- for the purpose and Sri Nitai Pal, the noted artist of Bengal who had sculptured the beautiful twin statues of Nitai-Gauranga for the temple at our Vrindavan Ashram, was commissioned to carve an image of Kali, to be installed on the Diwali day next year. Mataji Herself gave some indications of how the image should be made. While, for example, Kali is usually black, this Kali was to be made of the hue of the heavy grey-blue clouds, that gather before the monsoon breaks. The statue finally made out, was expected to be unusually alive and impressive. During the consecration, a strange thing happened. The priest, a Brahmachari of our Ashram who had been a student of science, noticed that the locket suspended on a golden chain with which the neck of the Goddess was adorned, vibrated distinctly as if the statue was breathing. When afterwards he carefully examined the image to make sure whether there was any physical cause to the phenomenon, he found to his amazement that the locket had got stuck at a point that was not yet quite dry.

Since the room in which the statue was installed seemed quite inadequate as a sanctuary of the Goddess, it was suggested that a temple should be built on the spot where Durga Puja had been celebrated last year. When the difficulties over the acquisition of the plot were finally overcome, the problem of funds remained to be solved. However, Kali Herself seemed to take the matter in hand!

Many years ago, a little boy called Manik Banerjee had said to the Goddess: "When I am grown up, I shall build a temple for you!" In his home at Barisal, a statue of Kali had been installed in a hut with a thatched roof. Manik's mother used to worship the Goddess every morning before she started doing her day's work. So the little boy also got used to worshipping the Goddess as his mother did. When much later he settled in Ranchi and built a house for himself, he felt that the time had come to fulfil his promise to Kali. He planned to build a temple right in front of his house. But he had a curious dream. Kali appeared to him and said, "Why build here? I am already in Ma Anandamayee Ashram." In his dream Manik Babu saw the Ashram of whose existence he was quite unaware. He disclosed his dream to a friend who was Mataji's devotee and who took him to the Ashram. Soon afterwards, namely in May 1958, when Mataji visited Ranchi, he was introduced to Her and in a long private interview told Her of his life-long devotion to Kali and of his dream. Mataji said: "Well, try to build the temple and then see what Kali Ma does." Actually Sri Manik Banerjee bore the entire cost of the temple, while construction of the beautiful large hall in front of it was financed by other devotees.

Swami Jnanananda Giri of Bholagiri Ashram at Hardwar was requested to supervise the building work. As usual, some difficulties arose and the actual expense far exceeded the estimate. But Kali Ma reassured the Swami in a dream, in which She showed him masses of gold coins and told him not to worry. On one occasion, the Swami felt so desperate that

he said to Kali, "Rather than wait till money is
provided, I shall sell all your jewellery and complete
the temple." That night he dreamt of a place covered
with a cloth. On removing it, he found an iron safe
that contained money. Kali said, "Take money from
here." "I am a Sannyasi," he replied, "I cannot take
anything, it has to be given." Kali then directed him
to approach Manik Babu again. During the Diwali
festival in 1962, the beautiful temple was consecrated
in Mataji's holy presence.

Eight

Ranchi, June 1965. One afternoon, while Sri Haribabaji was expounding the Gita between 5 and 6
p.m., Mataji saw a man with long white beard, who
had the appearance of a Rishi (sage), looking through
the window. She called one of the Brahmacharis
and drew his attention to this and he also was able to
see the venerable old man. Just outside the hall,
under a spreading banyan tree, there is a tomb of
Mohammedan saint who is supposed to have been a
"siddha fakir." It is possible that he was the one
whom Mataji saw looking in through the window
that day. A sum was given to the attendant of the
grave to perform a special puja and distribute the
prasada to the Mohammedan devotees.

Nine

Varanasi, Oct. 21, 1965. Mataji arrived at Varanasi
where Kali Puja was celebrated on Diwali Day. There
is a history to this particular puja. About 35 years
ago, when Mataji lived in Dacca, the grandson of
one of Her oldest devotees, Nishi Kanta Mitra, was
suffering from an abcess in his ear. The sick child
was then about eight months old, and the doctors

took a very serious view of his condition. *Mataji, at Her own place, picked up a needle and scratched the back of Her hand with it It was later found that the abscess had burst at about the same time. The child was saved.*

Mataji had enjoined on the family to perform Kali Puja every year on the day Diwali was celebrated in grateful commemoration of the child's recovery.

The child, when grown-up, had for a long time desired to have this puja performed in Mataji's presence. This year at last, he got the opportunity to arrange for it in our Varanasi Ashram. The scratch on Mataji's hand is still discernible.

Ten

Varanasi, Oct. 26. A strange little incident occurred during a Narayana puja at the residence of the architect of the Annapoorna Temple of our Ashram, Sri Manmohan Ghosh, a devotee of many years' standing. Mataji was sitting in the open courtyard watching the ceremony. One of the attending girls saw a small insect on Mataji's *asana* and wanted to remove it, when Mataji firmly caught hold of her wrist and told her to leave the insect where it was. After a little while, another girl approached Mataji and, seeing the insect, tried to brush it away. Mataji again prevented this. When a similar attempt was made for the third time, Mataji took the towel with which Her head was covered, carefully placed the insect on it, and put it on the shelf that was near Her head. The insect had become completely still by this time and Mataji drew someone's attention to it, remarking that it was in samadhi (deeply absorbed in meditation), as it were. After the puja, which lasted for three hours, Mataji took the towel from the shelf and, looking at the insect intently, said that it had left the body. She showed it to several of the people present. After cautiously wrapping it up in a towel, She summoned Narayan Swamiji who was asked to take the tiny creature to the Ganga and give it jal-samadhi, wrapt in the cloth that Mataji had worn on Her head. Who can tell who comes to Mataji in what guise? This is one of thousands of mysterious incidents that constantly take place around Her.

Eleven

Varanasi, Oct. 27. Mataji with a large party entrained for village Suriya near Hazaribagh Road Railway Station, reaching there the next morning. On the journey, Narayan Swami caught severe cold and on arrival at Hazaribagh Road, he had very high fever and breathing trouble. The attending physician diagnosed broncho-pneumonia. The Swami, an old man, was bed-ridden for the next few days and Mataji would go and see him daily, giving directions about treatment and diet. But lo and behold, on the first evening of the Samyam Vrata, he at Mataji's sugges-tion, gave an interesting lecture with a clear voice and with hardly a cough to disturb it. This verily was an unexpected speedy recovery, to say the least of it.

Twelve

One day at Suriya, when Mataji went round inspect-ing the preparations for *Samyam Vrata*, She saw a long row of hired tape-cots lined up in the open, ready to be put into the tents for use of the *vratis*. She advised that the cots should be put into the sun and sugar sprinkled on them to make sure that they

were free from troublesome insects like bugs. She
then related a story from Her early life. When She
stayed at Ashtagram with Bholanath, She once visited
Her home at Vidyakut (Mataji was then about 19 or
20 years old). There were innumerable bed-bugs in
the cots. Mataji watched the women trying various
remedies, with very little success though, to get rid
of the bugs. So She finally devised Her own cure.
When the whole family went away on a visit, She put
all the cots into the sun and sprinkled plenty of sugar
on them. This attracted large black ants which ate
up the eggs and perhaps also the smaller bugs, while
the bigger ones fled away. In any case, after three
days there was not a single bug left.

Thirteen

At the collective midnight meditation that always
marks the climax and end of Samyam Vrata satsang,
a Narayan Shila was enthroned on the dais near
Mataji's seat. This was an innovation. After the
meditation, Mataji said: "In future, whenever this
particular sort of Narayan Shila is available, you
may perform your Samyam Mahavrata in front of
Him."

This particular Narayan Shila has a story of its
own. When on Aug. 14, 1965, Mataji on Her way
from Dehradun to Jodhpur, halted in Vrindaban for
a day, a man connected with our Ashram told Her
that he had recently found a Narayan Shila on the
road while going round the temples of Vrindaban,
Although not a Brahmin (only a Brahmin is allowed
to worship a Narayan Shila), he had picked it up and
taken it with him. It then occurred to him that the
raised spot near Mataji's house in the Vrindaban

Ashram, where twelve Sannyasis had planted twelve tulsi shrubs, would be the suitable abode for the Shila. He had therefore buried it in the earth below those plants. Mataji asked him to bring the Shila to Her. Some of the people present were of the opinion that it was an ordinary stone, but Mataji had the *khayal* that it was a Narayan Shila. She washed and cleaned it with Her own hands and three chakras (circular signs) were found on the stone. Mataji then gave the Shila to one of the Ashram girls and asked her to do puja regularly and offer *bhoga* (food) to it.

Fourteen

After the *Samyam Saptaha* was over, Mataji remained in Suriya, Hazaribagh, for another eight days. During this period, She used to go for walks in the open fields twice daily. She would sometimes walk into the compounds of neighbouring villagers, talk to them and give them "Rama Nama" in Her own unique way. "Which of God's name do you like best?" She asked. "We like all of them," they replied. "But which of them do you repeat?" Much to Her surprise, they could not answer Her question. Mataji stretched out three fingers of Her right hand and pointing to each of them, said: "This is Rama, this is Krishna, this is Siva. Now catch hold of one." The next day She again went to see the villagers and sang "Rama Nama" to them and made them repeat every line after Her. Some of the people became friendly and brought vegetables, fruits and sugarcanes from their fields for Mataji, which She distributed. On the last day, She went to say good-bye to them calling them loudly by names until one by one they

came out of their houses and bade tearful good-bye
to Her.

Fifteen

Kankhal, April 1967. One day a touching little
incident took place. An old woman came and, to the
amusement of the congregation did pranama to an
American lady who was sitting near Mataji's empty
chair. When, towards the end of *darshan* time, the
old woman went up to Mataji and caught hold of her
feet, which is forbidden, she was severely rebuked
by those sitting nearby. To comfort her, Mataji patted
her and said, "What a joyful face you have! How
simple you are. This is why I could pick you out
from the crowd." Mataji then asked her name and
address, about her family, etc. Her name was Simladevi and she stayed at Harki Pauri in Hardwar.
Someone then told Mataji that Simladevi had bowed
to the American lady. At this Mataji told Simladevi:
"You have done the right thing. There is only Janar-
dana, none else. To whomever you bow, you bow
only to Him. Even animals, trees, stones — all are
He." It then came to light that Simladevi had fasted
all day, as she had decided to eat only after having
Mataji's *darshan*. In the morning, she had tried in
vain for it; now at last she had succeeded. Mataji
gave her a big *papita* and a bag full of oranges,
saying, "You have not taken even a piece of fruit all
day, now go home and eat all these." Then She
added, "You say you have four sons but no daughter.
Tell your husband that today, on New Year's day,
you got a daughter. I am your daughter. A mother
never forgets her daughter. Come and see me again."

Needless to say, Simladevi was beaming with happiness and paradoxically, moved to tears by Mataji's affection.

Sixteen

A young married woman would, under the slightest instigation, go into samadhi, or, rather, into what people called 'samadhi'. On such occasions she appeared lifeless, her limbs turning cold. Once this happened in Mataji's presence. Mataji at once understood what the matter was with the girl. She whispered a 'mantra' into her ear. And what was the 'mantra'? "You will very soon receive a letter from your husband." Ever since that day, the samadhi of the young woman never occurred again and her behaviour became normal.

Seventeen

Here is another incident of a different category altogether. A young man used to have visions of various kinds. He would, for instance, witness Sri Krishna tell Arjuna the Bhagavad Gita. He was profoundly moved by these visions. Tears would constantly stream down his eyes. When he narrated all these to Mataji, She told him: "Don't lose your self-control. Seekers after truth must never be overpowered by anything. Fully conscious and wide awake, with the attitude of a spectator, they must watch everything that happens."

Eighteen

One day a married woman came and lamented to Mataji, "Ma, in my home nobody approves of puja, japa, meditation and the like. My husband, my father-in-law, and all the rest of the members in the family, including my brother-in-law, are opposed to it What am I to do?" Mataji said: "You observe so many religious vows in your homes; don't you keep a fast on Tuesday and fast and do puja all night on Siva-ratri? Will you try to take up the following practice, mother? One day in a month, from morning till night, regard everyone as a manifestation of God. Your husband, your father-in-law, your brother-in-law — consider them to be God in different guises. That day, look upon your children as child Krishna and Kumari Devi. Whoever comes to your house, be he a guest, a beggar, a hawker, treat him as a form of Narayana. If on that day you are visited by any sorrow or trouble, welcome them as messengers of the Lord. By continuing with this practice, you will find circum-stances becoming normal and favourable to the worship of God. First of all, do this once every month, then once a week and you will observe that the happiness you feel on that day will influence all the rest of the week." Mataji continued: "Everyone should advance along one particular line. He who takes the path trodden by the lover of God, will realize Him as the blissful embodiment of Supreme Love. He who takes the path of Knowledge, will realize Him as Knowledge Itself as the formless Brahman. Just as one and the same individual is son, husband and father, so the One Brahman is Being, Consciousness, Bliss. From whichever angle a person approaches God, he will assuredly find Him, the One. If he progresses by yoga, he will realize eternal Union. He will have to go beyond the polarity of union and separation. And in the final attainment, the question of eternal and non-eternal, of beyond and not beyond, does not exist."

Nineteen

My husband's weak health was a matter of constant worry to me. With a view to invoking Mother's grace, I used to worship Her day and night for my husband's speedy recovery. In the meantime, I was asked by someone to pray directly before Mataji for his health. It was in the year 1959 that I made up my mind to beg to Mataji to cure my husband.

Luckily, Mataji came to Etawah in February 1960 and I decided to go and see Her there. It was my first private visit to Her. I quietly approached Her as a petitioner; but no sooner did I enter the room than both the manner and content of all that I wanted to say completely vanished from my mind. To my utter surprise, I found that the mental fog in which I had been enveloped, dissolved at the radiant smile of Ma. On Her asking me about my problem, I found myself speechless. Somehow I regained my original composure and told Her that I wanted to see my husband cured of the serious disease he was suffering from. Ma with Her usual ineffable sweet voice advised me to have faith in God and pray to Him for my husband. Although there was nothing new in Her advice, yet Her words were spoken in such a sympathetic tone that I had the experience of drinking in Mother's infinite compassion flowing freely from Her lustrous eyes. Soon I reached the state of oneness where Ma was mine and I was Hers completely. It made me feel as if Mataji had yielded to my wish and my husband was shortly after completely cured. Thereafter I would go nowhere else for his treatment.

Twenty

Vrindaban, Nov. 67. During *Matri Satsang,* the last half hour of the evening session of each day of *Samyam Saptaha,* Mataji sometimes replied to questions and sometimes related interesting incidents from Her life. The first three days, She gave part of Her time to Pd. Kapindraji, the well-known witty expounder of the Ramayana, who kept everyone amused and relaxed after the many serious and thought-provoking discourses of the day. On the 11th night, Pd. Kapindraji left for Delhi and promised to return on the 13th but he did not come. On the 14th night at the end of the programme, he suddenly emerged out of the crowd. Although Mataji requested him to have his meal and take rest as he had just arrived, he insisted on ascending the dais. *He then related that when he and five other persons had left for Delhi by Jeep at midnight on the 11th, he himself drove. As he was rather sleepy, the Jeep got out of control and fell into a ravine, 50 ft. deep. However, as if by miracle, nobody was hurt and even the Jeep remained intact, so that they could proceed to their destination. His daughter began to shriek with fear and then shouted: "Ma has come!" Kapindraji said: "Yes, Ma is here." He could see Her distinctly standing in front of him, only She seemed much taller than usual.*

Mataji: But how did you lift the jeep out of the abyss?

Kapindraji: You yourself lifted the wheels of the jeep, I saw it clearly. You saved us, you did everything.

Mataji: There is only One. God saved you. Since you have faith in this little girl, He appeared to you in Her shape to save you.

Twentyone

Vrindaban, Dec. 66. One day in the evening when Mataji came out for letting people have her *darshan,* two gentlemen arrived from outside. One is a physician, the other a former politician. After some time, Mataji asked everyone to disperse as She wanted to talk to her guests in private. After the interview, the physician gentleman narrated the following incidents connected with Mataji.

"I was very sceptical at first," he told, "and to begin with, came to confound Mataji with difficult questions. But She took me for a drive and on the way all my problems dissolved as if by miracle. Another time, I brought with me a Swamiji who had no faith at all in Her. He had devoted three whole days in formulating seven questions which he felt certain She would be unable to answer. When we arrived, Mataji asked me to accompany Her on a drive for ten minutes. "Of course," I thought, "this is how She is going to evade Swamiji." But ten minutes later, She told me She had to return in order to keep Her appointment with Swamiji. "Do you want to talk to me alone or in public?" She asked him. "In public," he said and then put his first question to which he received an appropriate answer. Then the second and the third, and every time Mataji replied without any hesitation whatsoever. Finally, Swamiji said, "I humbly beg your pardon for having doubted you. With great care, working for three whole days, I

prepared seven questions. I have nothing more to
ask, for you have already answered all other questions
as well." And ever since the Swami is one of Her
devoted followers.

Chapter Five

"I STAY IN BHADAINI KALI TEMPLE"

Varanasi in the month of May is nobody's haven due to oppressive and unbearable heat. Those who visit this holy city during this time of the year take back many happy memories along with the memory of intense heat. But I shall remember the month of May 1952 to the end of my life for no other reason than an unforgettable incident. Let me begin from the beginning.

I came to Varanasi from Calcutta in March 1951 with a friend with the intention of building up a practice in Ayurvedic medicine. We hired a room in Sonarpura area, made plans, started collecting tools of trade; but one day a midnight telegram nipped our project in the bud. The telegram was addressed to my friend from an acquaintance in Bombay inviting him there for a prospective job. My friend forgetting all about our well thought-out plan, decided to proceed at once to Bombay not probably for the allurement of a good job but mainly to get away from the scorching heat of Varanasi. I was thus left alone to brood over the plan of becoming a practitioner in Ayurvedic medicine, but the prospect looked dimmer day by day and ultimately I had to abandon the idea. I then started looking for a job.

It was a part of my daily routine to go and sit each afternoon with a sizeable crowd on the spacious steps of the famous Dasaswamedh Ghat and hear discourses on Tulsi's *Ramayana,* as a part of daily *satsang.* One day I went a bit early to the *satsang* and found that after sometime, a respectable-looking gentleman seated himself just beside me. After some routine talk about weather, etc. he inquired about my vocation. I told him my tale of woe, adding that I was in search of a job so that I could find means for staying permanently at Varanasi. He said he was looking for a man who could act as a care-taker of his house with an attached garden situated at the Gurudham area of the city. The owner also informed that the house was untenanted and that his purpose of coming to Varanasi from Calcutta was to appoint a caretaker, who would have to stay in and look after the house, on a monthly allowance of Rs.100/-, until the house was sold out. I made a quick decision and, like a drowning man, readily offered myself to be the care-taker of his house. The deal was struck then and there and I was installed in the new assignment from the very next day. It was middle of April 1951.

The house I had to look after was a fairly big one with a spacious compound in front of it and a garden on its Southern side containing about a dozen mango and guava trees and also some beds of roses and other flower plants. It was part of my daily duty to water the plants myself, although there was a paid Mali (gardener) to keep the garden neat and clean by weeding out dried leaves, etc. In summer months, it was very refreshing to pass the mornings and evenings in the garden in the cool shade of trees facing the roses in full bloom with a riot of colours.

A year rolled by in placid peace. In came the oppressive month of May 1952, but it was a memorable month in my life. One evening after sun-set, I was as usual reclining on a charpoy with an English magazine in my hand and enjoying the cool breeze.

Suddenly a sweet girlish voice from behind startled me. On turning back I found a girl of not more than 15 or 16 years of age standing with a smiling face and shining eyes. As I was sitting with my back to the main gate, I could hardly be aware of her silent entrance or her stealthy approach towards me. The colour of her face was blackish and one end of her red-bordered white sari was wound round her slender waist. One thing about her which would at once attract everybody's notice was her wonderful and abundant mass of black hair flowing loosely down her back. Her feet were bare and two white glass bangles adorned her wrists. From her simple dress and appearance, she seemed to belong to some working class family, but in that scarlet hue of the setting sun she appeared to me simply wonderful.

Noticing my slight embarrassment and mute admiration in my eyes, she asked me in a melodious tone, "Babuji, won't you give me a couple of ripe mangoes?" My first reaction was indirect refusal which I repented later in leisure. I replied pointing to a mango-laden tree, "Look, the mangoes are still green. How can I give you ripe mangoes?" However, she brushed aside my reply and unwounding a portion of her waist-bound sari and stretching the two ends of it with her two hands, she appealed, "Please give, Babuji, give. Haven't you got some in your room?" Her mention of 'room' made me remember with a

guilty conscience the three ripe mangoes I had
gathered that very morning while strolling in the
garden, mangoes that had fallen from the trees at
night. I asked her to wait a minute and ran to my
room. Holding two mangoes in my hand, I returned
to her. Her face brightened with beatific smile and,
exhibiting child-like simplicity and haste to grab a
priceless thing, she stretched out the portion of her
cloth still held by her hands and gleefully said, "Drop
them here, Babuji." When I did so, she pointed with
her right hand towards the rose-beds and said in the
same sweet appealing tone, "Now please give me
some roses, Babuji." I was going to refuse but restrain-
ing myself I replied, "You can pluck a few yourself,
if you like." But surprisingly she refused to do the
plucking herself and asked me instead to do it for
her. I then plucked a few roses of different colours
and dropped them into her folded palms. She seemed
immensely delighted, and as she was about to retreat,
I just halted her by raising my hand and then put to
her a number of questions one after another: "Where
are you coming from? Do you happen to stay near
by? Are you a neighbour of ours? Where do you
actually stay?" With a twinkle in her eyes, she answered my last question, *"I stay in Bhadaini Kali
Temple."* So saying, she turned back and virtually
ran towards the gate and vanished without giving
me an opportunity of asking any further question.

For a few moments, I was in a trance as it were,
and when I came to my own, I ran to the front gate
hoping to find her somewhere near by. But my search
was in vain and, strangely enough, the few passers-
by whom I met on the road, denied having seen such
a girl in the locality.

On returning to my resting place in the garden, I started pondering over the dramatic happening of the last half an hour. The more I thought about it, the more mysterious it seemed to me. The sudden appearance of an unknown and uncommon girl, her unearthly appearance, manner, gaiety and talk — all seemed on closer scrutiny to be surrounded with mystery. And take her last words. "I stay in Bhadaini Kali Temple." At first I took it as an innocent joke because during my stay of over a year in Varanasi, I had occasions to visit all the Kali temples of the city. But I had never heard of the existence of a Kali temple in Bhadaini area and, strangely enough, this area is not very far off from the house in which I live. Was then her statement nothing but a juvenile prank or was it a spontaneous truthful admission? I decided to verify it in order to satisfy my two-fold curiosity that arose in my mind to confirm the existence of a Kali temple at Bhadaini which in turn might lead to a possible clue to knowing more about that mysterious girl. With these twin resolves in my mind, I set out to pursue my task from the very next morning. For one week I virtually ransacked the whole area of Bhadaini, visited every nook and corner, pestered many people of the locality, asked the Pujaris of the two well-known and important Kali temples — Panchakote Kali temple and Cooch Behar Kali temple — situated within the radius of a mile but none could vouchsafe the existence of a Kali temple at Bhadaini and everybody denied having any knowledge about it. All my labour was thus futile, and this disheartened me, more so because I harboured a feeling in my innermost heart that there was a ring of truth in what the girl told me about her abode. Although the search was abandoned, a faint hope, however, lingered in my mind that some day the girl would re-visit the garden and ask for mangoes or flowers. But the days rolled by without any sign of my cherished hope being fulfilled.

Then happened the most incredible incident three months later on the Janmashtami Day (Birthday of Lord Sri Krishna). As on other auspicious days, an early morning dip in the Ganga on the Janmashtami Day is a must. On that day, I decided to have a dip in the Anandamayee Ghat adjacent to Sri Sri Ma Anandamayee Ashram at Bhadaini. I started at day-break and had a dip in the Ganga at that particular Ghat. When I was ascending the steps after the bath, an unbelievable spectacle caught my eyes. From the window of the Annapoorna Temple of the Ashram, which overlooks the Ganga, two white hands with spotlessly white conch-shell bangles on, were found to be waving as if sportingly, but to me they looked like beckoning me to come nearer. It lasted only a few moments after which the hands were withdrawn to my utter bewilderment. I stood rooted to the spot oblivious of the world around me. With the sun just up in the sky, it was neither a dream nor a hallucination. Could it then be a purposeful action of a woman devotee doing her daily morning salutation to the rising sun? That was at least the reasonable explanation one could give to that unusual happening. With a decision in my mind to know what it was all about, I went inside the Ashram and met a Brahmachari in the inside courtyard. Looking at the bundle of wet clothes in my hand he thought I wanted to do pranam

to the deities in the temple as many people do after a
bath in the Ganga and so he directed me to the stair-
case leading to the first floor of the building wherein
lies the Annapoorna Temple just by the side of the
Ganga. Standing in front of the temple door, I looked
inside and found a pujarı (priest) sitting in deep
meditation in front of the several deities installed
there. There was none else inside the room and
certainly not any female devotee, the object of my
exploration. I then directed my attention to the
deities. On the left-hand side, two big Shivalingas
and several Narayanshilas were found installed. On
the right- hand side of the room, I found a big glass
case on a raised pulpit of marble stone. To have a
clearer view of the deities inside the glass case, I
moved a step or two nearer the temple door and
found images of Devi Annapoorna and Lord Siva
made of some burnished metal like gold. I closed my
eyes and did obeisance to them. On opening my eyes,
my gaze was fixed on a jet-black image of Mother
Kali, on the right-hand side of the glass case, standing
on the breast of a lying Shivamurti. At once a thought
flashed across my mind. Was this then the much
sought-after Kali Temple of Bhadaini as mentioned
by that mysterious girl? This must be the one, I felt
convinced, as there was none other. But where was
that girl who had mentioned this as her place of
abode? I reasoned that she must be somewhere here
in this Ashram. With a ruffled mind, I hurriedly ran
downstairs and made inquiries about the girl but
everybody was emphatic in his reply that no such
girl of my description did ever stay in that Ashram.
Someone even sarcastically remarked that the girl I

was searching for was nothing but a figment of my imagination. But how could I convince him that the girl I had met in my garden was not a fanciful object but very much a living human being of flesh and blood. I thought it better to give up that futile attempt. I came out of the Ashram and took the way to my home with a heart elated and satisfied at the dramatic discovery of the Bhadaini Kali Temple which solved at least one mystery and that discovery generated in my mind a faint ray of hope of resolving the mystery of the girl as well as of the owner of those two waving hands. Needless to say, I observed the Janmashtami festival with a joyful heart.

For the next few days the indelible memory of that inconceivable vision of the two beautiful waving hands haunted me day and night. Those hands couldn't belong to that elusive girl. Then whom did those hands belong to — Devi Annapoorna, Mother Kali or somebody else? Whoever it might be, it was a mystery beyond my comprehension. I only prayed to God to reveal the truth to me someday.

A week later, I went to the Ashram and the person I met first was no other than its Secretary who was popularly known as Kamalda (Virjananda). Tauntingly he smiled and said, "Are you not the same person who inquired the other day about a mysterious girl? Could you find her out?" I replied in the negative. He then said, "What do you do? Can't you help us in the Ashram work?" I replied, "I can, but before that I want to have a *darsan* of Ma. Is She here?" "Yes," he said, "She is here. You can wait in that hall down there on the side of the Ganga where She will come after a while." On entering the hall (which was subsequently demolished after it was damaged by flood water), I found about thirty persons sitting on a duree — men on one side and women on the other, all expectantly waiting for Ma. I quietly sat down at the rear and waited. After about 15 minutes, all stood up in reverence as Ma entered the hall. At first sight Ma appeared to me like a goddess just descended from heaven. She glided past me and took the seat allotted to her at the top end of the hall. She was dressed all in white and a white chaddar (wrapper made of cotton) covered her body including her hands. A few minutes passed in blissful silence and then Ma asked an Ashram girl to sing bhajans. As she finished one bhajan and was about to start the second, Ma brought out, from underneath the wrapper, her hand and started adjusting the garment on her shoulders. Seeing those hands with conch-shell bangles on, my heart leaped to my throat as it were, because those were the hands I had no difficulty whatsoever in recognizing, hands that had waved outside the Annapoorna temple the other day while I was ascending the steps of the nearby bathing ghat. The impact of that revelation was stunning and overwhelming for me. The owner of those two divine hands was none else but Ma Anandamayee who through her infinite compassion and grace revealed to me the identity of the owner of the waving hands. My heart overflowed with joy as the revelation had a special message for me, a message of Mother's boundless grace and ineffable compassion. I then got up from my seat, drew near Ma and without a word prostrated myself before her with a heart full of gratitude and reverence.

I now leave it to you all to establish the identity of that mysterious girl. To me, her identity stood fully revealed. After meeting Ma, I had no doubt whatsoever in my mind that it was Ma herself who kindly visited my garden out of sheer compassion in the guise of an unknown and uncommon girl. You may of course draw your own conclusions. But I shall die with my own.*

JAI GURU, JAI MA

Words of Ma

Wherever God may keep you at any time, from there itself must you undertake the pilgrimage to God-realization. In all forms, in action and non-action is He, the One Himself.

While attending to your work with your hands, keep yourself bound to Him by sustaining japa, the constant remembrance of Him in your heart and mind. In God's empire, it is forgetfulness of Him that is detrimental. The way to Peace lies in the remembrance of Him and of Him alone.

A traveller on the path to God-realization has to obey his Guru's instructions so that his journey may be crowned with success. However, in a case where there are no such instructions, one should, according to the dictates of one's heart, keep oneself occupied in calling out to God in prayer or meditation. If someone prays to Him with a sincere and simple heart, God will fulfil his cherished desire. To yearn for Him with his whole being is man's duty.

As narrated to the Author by a devotee Sri B.K. Guha

Chapter 6

FLASHES OF MOTHER'S LILA OF COMPASSION

One
(As recorded by Didi Gurupriya Devi in her Diary)

18.1.59.   Three days ago, Mataji went to the hospital to see Mukti Maharaj. Dr. Radhakrishnan, the Vice-President of India, is at present admitted into the Presidency Hospital of Calcutta, as he had to undergo an operation. Immediately after the operation, Mataji had the special *khayal* (thought) to go and see him. Dr. Radhakrishnan was not then conscious. No visitors were allowed to enter the patieint's room while he was in that condition. But since Mataji wanted to see him, Dr. B.C. Das Gupta took her with him to the patient's cabin. The two nurses in charge of Dr. Radhakrishnan were unwilling to permit her to step into the room. But since Dr. Das Gupta had brought her, they could not prevent it. Having no alternative left to them, the two nurses entered with Mataji and joining hands, stood on both sides of the bed. They obviously tried to keep Mataji from touching the patient. But Mataji some-how put her hand below theirs and, without anyone noticing it, touched the bedsheet. When on recovering consciousness Dr. Radhakrishnan received the

news of Mataji's visit, he expressed great joy and
feelingly requested a number of people to convey
his deep gratitude to Her. It is difficult for us to
understand when, on whom and in what way Mataji
may bestow her grace. Nobody requested her to go
and see Dr. Radhakrishnan, nobody even mentioned
to Her that he was in the hospital, yet of Her own
accord, she came and blessed him. This is called
'ahetuki kripa' (unsolicited and causeless grace). Who
could have foretold what was written in Dr. Radhakrishnan's fate? (When Dr. Radhakrishnan recovered, he came to see Mataji and at his special request
Mataji once visited his residence in Delhi.).

Two

In this connection, another example of Mataji's
grace, without any visible cause or reason, comes to
my mind. Some time ago, a middle-aged woman
without any means of her own, came to live in our
Varanasi Ashram. Although her name was Kamala,
Mataji called her "Gopal's Mother", since she kept
an image of the child — Krishna (Gopal) with her,
whom she worshipped. She became a regular inmate
of the Ashram. I was hardly acquainted with her,
but I noticed that Mataji showered Her grace with
great lavishness on the woman. One day Mataji said
to me: "Gopal's mother is a very fine person. Moreover, she is very neat and clean in her work." I felt
amused at Mataji's praising her so highly and replied:
"Really? I have failed to notice it so far." Mataji
contradicted, saying: "May be. But remember that
the poor woman has no one and nothing to call her
own. She can do only as much work as she is capable
of "

One night Mataji appeared to be a little unwell. At about midnight, she suddenly remembered Gopal's mother and sent for her at that very moment As soon as she came and stood before Mataji, the latter gave her a broad smile and asked, "Well, how do you like staying in the Ashram?" Gopal's mother did not reply at all cheerfully. Mataji listened attentively and then said: "Look, in the Ashram you are living on the banks of the Ganges. Do your worship and prayers (sadhan-bhajan) and for the rest, try to give whatever service you can. All the Ashramites will take care of you, and you also try to look after them just a little. How does this sound to you?" Mataji's loving words seemed suffused with compassion.

A few days later, when Mataji's health had improved to some extent, she went to Gopal's mother's room and arranged every detail in it — the place of her worship, the place where she slept, etc. Our gracious Mother confers Her grace without any cause or reason, unexpectedly. Who can tell by what good works in her former births, Gopal's mother earned the privilege of finding refuge with Mataji and of becoming the recipient of Her boundless grace?

Three

4.2.59.   This afternoon, after partaking of our midday meal, we started by car for Lucknow. Many devotees were waiting all along the road to have Mataji's *darsan,* not heeding the discomforts that this long waiting caused. After we passed Unnao District, Mataji pointed to a nearby village, exclaiming, "Look, Didi, what a lovely little village!" I saw a

cluster of mud-houses nestling among trees but could
not discover anything extraordinary about that small
village. When a little later I heard Mataji remark
again, Aren't those trees beautiful!", I said: "All
right, let us go and see them from close." Mataji
replied with some hesitation, "But the car has taken
us quite a distance from there by now." "What does
it matter?" I put in eagerly. "Let us go there, please."
The driver was asked to turn the car and drive back.
When we had recovered a short distance, I saw that
there was an opening in the middle of the fields and
the car could take us right into the village. As soon
as we had reached it, Mataji got out of the car and
walked with great speed straight towards one of the
houses. I asked, "Ma, where are the trees of which
you talked?" But instead of giving me an answer,
Mataji said, "Bring all the flower-garlands and the
basket of fruits that are in the car!" I did as I was
bidden and carrying the flowers and fruits I started
running behind Mataji. Soon I saw a pond near a
house and on the banks of the pond, there were two
young trees — one a banyan and the other a margosa
tree, growing side by side. Mataji went close to the
two trees and started fondling and caressing them
with so much affection that we all stood speechless,
staring in amazement at this unusual scene. Pressing
the forehead and her face again and again against
the two tree-trunks, She said, "Well, well, so you
have brought this body here to see you!" As far as I
could judge, the two trees that brought Mataji so
dramatically to them did not seem to have anything
special about them, outwardly at least, neither were
they particularly strong, nor had they many leaves,

nor were they well shaped; yet invisible to us, there must surely have been something about them that made Mataji eager to come to them and bless them so abundantly.

By and by, the villagers came out of their houses and crowded round us. Mataji asked them, "What is the name of your village?" "Bhawanipur", was the reply. Mataji: "Who had planted these two trees?" Someone said: "Dwarka." We were also told that the master of the house was not at home. Everyone pointed to his wife. Standing close to the trees, Mataji said: "Take great care of these two trees and worship them. It will be for your good." Then Mataji with Her own hands decorated the trees with all the garlands we brought and distributed among the villagers whatever fruits She had.

She then asked the mistress of the house, "Have you a daughter?" The poor woman could not understand what Mataji was driving at. In the fashion of village women, she had a long veil drawn over her face. Seeing all that Mataji was doing, she stood quite perplexed. Addressing her again, Mataji said, "I have made you my mother," and pointing to Herself: "This is your little daughter!" While walking back to the car, Mataji uttered: "Margosa and Banyan — Hari and Hara!" I asked: "Have you given the trees these names? Fine." When we got into the car, the crowd had followed us there as well. I enjoined on them: "Plaster the space under those trees with mud." Mataji asked them: "Do you repeat God's holy name? Even though you may be able to do so daily, at any rate now and again perform puja and sing kirtan or religious songs under those trees."

The car started. "How surprising!" Mataji observed. "Those two trees were pulling this body towards them as human beings might. The car was carrying us away from them, but it was just as if they had caught hold of the chest and back of this body and dragged it backwards in their direction. This kind of thing has never happened before."

We tried hard to find out from Mataji who or what those two trees actually were. But Mataji gave no clear reply. It is difficult to foretell whether light will ever be thrown on this mysterious incident. Behind many of Mataji's apparently trifling actions, deep mystery lies hidden. What a great number of supernatural happenings occur in connection with Mataji! How many of them are we able to understand?

Four
(During Samyam Mahavrata at Ramnagar, Rishikesh from Apr. 13 — 22, 1959)

One evening toward the close of the function for that day, Mataji asked an old devotee to tell her about any strange experience he had had.

He narrated something like the following: Yesterday afternoon I went to have a bath in the Ganges, but as I walked back, I discovered that I had lost the key of my room. All searching proved futile. Here I was, pining to join the Satsang, but how could I enter the hall in wet clothes? Almost in tears I sat down on a stone, wondering how to open my room. Suddenly I felt someone was approaching. Looking up I saw a beautiful lady, dressed in a white sari and resembling our Ma, standing before me. She seemed to hail from the hills. "What is the matter?", she inquired. I told her of my trouble and she replied: "Your key may be in the water somewhere." She then took off her sandals and stepped into the Ganges. In no time did she come out of the water with my key in her hand. It seemed quite miraculous. I felt so enormously grateful, I could not help thanking her. "You çall me 'Mother' and thank me", she said, "go and wash your key; it is covered with sand." I obeyed, but when I turned round and looked up, the lady had vanished. How she could have disappeared so quickly I could not understand. In fact, there was something mysterious about the whole incident. I however opened my room and changed into dry clothes, but I did not go to the Satsang. I was deeply stirred. I had lost my key and my Mother had found it for me. But where was the key to my life? How could I open the door to my real being? I was tormented by this question and lay awake all night. When I related to Mataji about my strange experience, She asked a few questions about the beautiful lady and then said: "It was Mother Ganges who appeared to you." I said: "There was no one to be seen afterwards." Mataji remarked: "Where no one is, there is HE."

After the old gentleman had narrated his story, Mataji said: "This is why you take part in the Samyam Vrata — in order to find the key. This is why the function is held on the banks of a holy river, that you may find the real key that has remained lost through so many births. This is the place where the key can be found, Mother Ganges herself may come and give it to you."

Five

(As experienced by Vijayananda during Mother's Birthday celebrations in May 1959)

During the last night of Mother's birthday celebrations (or rather in the early morning) at the end of the Tithi Puja, everyone is allowed to go near her to do obeisance and offer flowers or whatever one chooses to offer. This can only be done one by one and as hundreds of people are present, it is bound to take a good deal of time. The mind would naturally wish that there should be some efficient organization keeping people in a queue and making them recede by a different way after doing their pranams. But in Mother's presence, discipline and organization from outside may be out of place and perhaps even harmful, for by it the free play of the Divine Power might be hampered through the rigidity of the human will. In fact on most occasions, without any organization, people walk upto Mother one by one in perfect order and in complete silence, but on this occasion in Dehradun, this was not the case.

I was present during that holy night at Kishenpur, and like everybody else, I also tried to approach Mother when the puja was over. On such nights, Mother usually lies on a couch, absolutely still and to all appearance far removed from all bodily consciousness. As soon as She returns to the normal state, offerings and salutations are stopped and Mother is led back to Her room.

I had brought a beautiful bouquet of flowers with a view to offering it to Mother. I tried first to follow one queue, but another one had formed from a different direction. After several unfruitful attempts, I at last managed to come near Mother with only three or four people in front of me. But at that moment, a few ladies rushed in and we were obliged to stand back. I then reflected that one should after all take things as they come on all occasions and thus remained aloof. At that very moment, Mother sat up. A human semi-circle was formed around Her to protect Her from the crowd. Offering and salutations had to stop. It looked as if the bouquet I had brought would not fulfil its purpose of existence.

A few minutes later, Mother rose. On such occasions, it takes some time before she fully recovers body-consciousness and She is led to Her room, supported by several persons. Two human walls are formed on both sides of Her way to enable Her to walk, undisturbed by the intruding crowd. Strangely enough, the spot where I stood aloof was just on Mother's way and between the human walls. *Mother advanced, facing exactly in my direction. I deposited the bunch of flowers at Her feet, made obeisance and stepped out of Her way.*

When afterwards I pondered over this incident, I realized that in that holy night, notwithstanding the variegated crowd and the confusion resulting therefrom I had had the chance to present my offerings to Mother in a unique and exceptional way, in fact, in precisely the manner that I preferred. Probably many other persons had similar experiences.

Six

(As recorded by Didi Gurupriya Devi in her Diary)

28.5.1952.   At the special request of Sri·Durga
Singhji, Raja Sahib of Solan, Mataji returned from
Jacko Hills of Simla to Solan today. In the evening,
something remarkable occurred that is worth recording. One of the Brahmacharis of our Ashram had a
talk with Mataji about his sadhana. Immediately
afterwards, Mataji called me: "Just imagine, Didi,"
she said, "What a strange thing has just happened!
The Brahmachari, although a disciple of Sri Devi
Giriji, asked this body what the object of his contem-
plation should be. To start with, this body had the
khayal to tell him he should proceed as he had been
instructed at the time of his initiation. He also explained clearly what kind of japa he was practising. All of
a sudden, I saw in that corner of the couch (Mataji
indicated the side where She usually keeps Her head
when lying) the figure of a person who with his raised
hand pointed to that spot. (A nice large picture
representing Mataji is kept there). He did so once.
While talking, I kept on casting glances at him. Once
again he distinctly pointed to the same spot." Mataji
laughed heartily when She added: "Who can tell,
perhaps he was drawing attention to your room,
Didi." I also joined·in the laughter and said: "How
very nice! No doubt he must have pointed to me!
But what was figure like?"

With a smile Mataji replied: "He looked like the
charioteer of Partha (Sri Krsna is described as the
charioteer of Partha (Arjuna) in the Bhagavad Gita).
He wore that kind of dress. He stood up very straight

and with His long arm that reached down to His knees, He pointed in that direction. Think of it, at first it did not strike me, but later it became clear that He appeared exactly in the place where the Srimad Bhagavat is being kept."

The Brahmachari was called and in Mataji's presence I told him all about the strange incident. He responded by saying: "Oh yes, I did notice that while talking, Mataji seemed, as it were, to have been preoccupied with other thoughts. The atmosphere here in the room also became enchanted. As She spoke to me, Mataji's eyes twice wandered in that direction. But I could not see anything at all."

Without uttering a word, Mataji listened to our conversation, smiling gently. I then told the Brahmachari: "It is well known that Mataji does not always explain clearly what happens; there can, however, not be the shadow of a doubt that today Sri Krishna Himself has appeared and indicated to you by His gesture to contemplate Mataji as She is on that picture."

Finally Mataji said to the Brahmachari: "At any rate, you should do one thing: whenever you sit down for your meditation, first of all concentrate on that form of Sri Krishna and then, after doing obeisance to Him, contemplate whatever else it may be. For, He Himself has come today in that form to intimate to you what to do. This is why you should start your meditation by thinking of HIM!"

Seven

3.6.1952.   In the course of conversation, Mataji related something that had happened long, long ago.

At that time, Mataji and Bhaiji were staying in the vicinity of Dehradun. One day they went on foot to Uttarkashi. While trudging up a mountain path, Bhaiji felt exhausted due to extreme hunger and thirst. Only with great difficulty did he continue to walk. They were surrounded by mountains and dense forests, and there was not even a trace of human habitation. Suddently as if happening by Mataji's mere *khayal,* they saw a small boy walking straight towards them. He was carrying a large earthen vessel full of *khowa* (milk so boiled that it becomes solid, a kind of fresh cheese). How miraculous! After partaking of the khowa and drinking some water from the spring, Bhaiji felt much better. Later he told Mataji that he had never before eaten such wonderfully tasty khowa.

Eight

Now to another strange incident. Once when walking with Mataji near Dehradun on a hot day, Bhaiji felt exceedingly thirsty. Mataji too would have welcomed a drink of water. But at a moment's notice, she did no longer feel like drinking and simultaneously Bhaiji's inordinate thirst seemed quenched as well. Mataji said to Bhaiji, "Atal has offered some water-melon and this is how our thirst has been slaked." At that time, Atal da was hundreds of miles away in far off Bengal. Bhaiji made a note of the date and hour and later wrote to Atal da inquiring about the matter. He got the reply that since it was exceptionally hot day, he had at that very hou offered some melon-sherbat to Mataji's picture! Is there a limit to the variety of Mataji's lila? Hundreds of similar incidents occur at all times. How few of them come to our notice and how much of those that do come, are we capable of understanding?

Nine

Kali was the presiding deity of Bholanath's family. To perform Kali puja every year was therefore their family tradition. Bholanath and his brothers had to move from place to place on account of their various professions for which it was not always possible for them to get together even for the annual puja. The brothers therefore agreed to take turns in performing the puja. According to this arrangement, Bholanath had once performed the puja while he stayed in Bajitpur. Some miraculous incidents had taken place during that puja. Mataji was not very widely known at that time, which explains why the knowledge of those supernatural occurrences remained confined to a few people only.

After coming to Shahbagh Mataji, at the request of Bholanath and others, performed the Kali-puja in the year 1925. This was the first time that Mataji had publicly performed a puja with physical accessories.

A year passed and again the time for the annual Kali-puja drew near. This year had brought about many changes in the mode of her life. Firstly, she had become very widely known and Shahbagh was teeming with crowds every day. Secondly, she herself had begun to move freely amongst people. Moreover, in spite of frequent still states of samadhi and *bhava,* her behaviour was gradually getting nearer to the ordinary, so that she was becoming approachable to people. Thus, when a few days before the puja,

Bholanath requested her to perform it, she expressed her unwillingness, saying: "Do not request me to do these things any more. You can see for yourself that I am unable to perform any work." Seeing Mataji's unwillingness, and that it was not his turn to perform the family puja, Bholanath dropped the idea altogether.

A few days later, Mataji was going to Didi's house for bhoga. On the way, inside the carriage, she suddenly raised her hand and seemed to be looking at something. Later on, when she sat down for her meal, she again raised her arm in exactly the same manner and at once appeared as if she was far removed from her immediate surroundings. Just one day before Kali-puja, when Mataji and Bholanath had retired for the night, she asked him, "What was Bhudeb Babu talking to you about?" Bholanath was surprised because that afternoon B. Babu had asked him to request Mataji to perform the puja. Bholanath had declined, telling him of Mataji's unwillingness, and everyone had gone away disappointed that there would be no puja that year. Mataji had not met B. Babu, and of course after Bholanath's refusal, nobody had dared to request her again. Therefore Bholanath was amazed at her question. When he told her of his conversation with B. Babu, Mataji said, "Why don't you perform the puja yourself?" Interpreting this as her sanction for the puja, Bholanath immediately went outside and conveyed the good news to Baul Babu and Suren Babu (some of the first devotees and admirers of Mataji at Dacca) who were still there. As only one day remained to prepare for the puja, the image had to be fetched that very night and

all arrangements expedited. Now the question arose
as to the size of the image. Bholanath went to ask
Mataji. He found Her lying on the floor in a state of
deep samadhi. She was unable to speak and his
question remained unanswered. Here was an unexpected obstacle. Then it suddenly occurred to
Bholanath that the image should be as high as Mataji
had lifted Her arm while in the carriage and in Didi's
house. He then somehow managed to tilt up Her
body to sitting posture and held up Her arm. The
distance from the ground to Her uplifted hand
measured about 40 inches. Baul Babu and others
then went to town to procure an image of this size.
They found that all the images had been sold out
and that only one artist had a single image left.
Strangely and luckily it turned out to be of the exact
size, although the colour was a little unusual, being
more bluish than black. When Mataji saw the image,
She said that on the way to Didi's house, She had
'seen' a Kali-murti of this very size and hue, rushing
down from above as if to leap into Her arms. She
had again 'seen' this image at Didi's house. Kali was
wearing a large garland of bright red hibiscus flowers
and there was no Shiva under her feet.

    The arrangements for the puja proceeded in full
swing. Shahbagh was crowded with people. Midnight
drew near. There was not an inch of space in the
puja room. Mataji was in her own room, sitting in a
state of bhava, immovable and remote with fixed
and unseeing eyes and oblivious of her surroundings.
Bholanath somehow managed to guide her steps to
the pond, helped her to take a bath and change into
a new sari. He then brought her back and seated her

in front of the image. In the nearby room, people were singing kirtan. The atmosphere was fragrant with the scent of flowers and incense and the puja was performed with due rites.

Ten
(As narrated by Dr. C.H. Kuang)

I have had the good fortune of knowing Mother Anandamayi and Her beneficient influence for many years. I met Her first at the Raipur Ashram, Dehradun while I was on an educational tour through India. I vividly recollect this first darsan of Mother which has remained a very distinct and definite impression in my mind. It was about 1 p.m. on a day in January 1946 when the Manager of Roadways of Dehradun, who happened to be a devotee of Mother, very kindly arranged for me to go to the Raipur Ashram in his car. On arriving at the Ashram gate, I found thousands of men and women gathered round Mother. The hall was packed and I was unable to enter and therefore stood outside for about twenty minutes or so. It seemed to me that all men and women present were asking Mother to give them something of Her grace or blessing without making any effort themselves. It is true when we begin to seek Truth, we need a Guru to guide us safely through all sorts of obstacles and difficulties that have to be faced on the spiritual path. The Guru's grace is certainly needed by the aspirant. But this does not mean that disciples should sit idly by their Guru's side and expect to be pushed into Samadhi by some miracle. It is obvious that we have ourselves to walk every step of the spiritual path. God resides within every being, the Purusha in his perfection ever exists. If we practise meditation, we shall see God. As Mother says, "Meditation is the real form of worship and formal ceremonies are but passing phases."

When at 1-30 p.m. Mother came out of the hall and stepped into a car, I gave up all hope of meeting Her, for I had come without having any acquaintance with Her, all alone with my burning heart in search of Truth. *At that very moment, Mother called me by raising Her hand and invited me to get into the car and sit by Her side.* We drove straight to the railway station. Mother was kind enough to consent to my travelling to Hardwar with Her in the same compartment, along with Mr. J.C. Mukerji, an Advocate of the High Court, Allahabad. We three were sitting together undisturbed all the way to Hardwar. I utilized every minute of the journey to benefit by putting question after question on Indian philosophy, religion and systems of Yoga. Mr. Mukerji acted as an interpreter. Mother's replies to my questions gave me great satisfaction. She has had no school education at all, but Her knowledge is so profound and wide. Of course a person who gives spiritual instruction should not have mere book knowledge but must have first-hand spiritual experience. Don't we read in Shri Ramkrishna's sayings that a teacher who undertakes to expound religion from book-learning is like a man who undertakes to describe Banaras after having seen merely a map of the sacred city. Mother also gave me some advice concerning meditation.

When we got down at Hardwar railway station, an old Muslim gentleman came and bowed and prostrated himself before Mother. Mr. Mukerji remarked: "Chou, just see how this old Muslim gentleman, who is a professor of philosophy of the Allahabad University, puts his head on the ground before Mother. How great Mother is." Mother allowed me to accompany Her to the Dharmasala for some time and then I had to take leave of Her, as my train for Lahore was due at 6 p.m. or so. Before I parted from Her, Mother told me again that if I had any spiritual experience, I should write to Her. I spontaneously responded by saying, "Will you accept me as your disciple?" She just kept quiet with a smile on Her lips. The sun was setting on the Western Himalayas when I returned to the station and Mother strolled to the Ganges.

Eleven

(As narrated by Sri P.M. Verma)

During the last five years, I have had more occasions of Mother's darshan during Her visits to Allahabad, although every time I preferred to go to Her incognito in the sense that I did not seek to be introduced to Her. I felt She had always known me, and She fully satisfied every test by which I thought I could fathom Her depths as the Supreme Incarnation of the Universal Mother. To illustrate my point with a few specific instances, let me first begin with that fateful day, Jan. 30, 1948, when the news was broadcast through the Radio at about 8 p.m. of the passing away of the Father of the Nation. I was at that time sitting in the Mother's camp in the Maghmela in

Allahabad along with many other Bhaktas awaiting the arrival of the Mother. It was a very unusual feature that evening that kirtan had started in the camp where She gave audience, but She had not come even at that late hour. Somebody said that Mother was taking rest on Her return from Jhusi. A good number of the Bhaktas left after waiting for more than one hour. Those that kept waiting and I was one of them — were taken aback to receive a rather peremptory direction from some whitecaps, who entered the camp, to stop the kirtan immediately as the news had come of Mahatmaji's passing away. As I left the tent, the idea uppermost in my mind was that Mother had not come that day to 'give darshan, because She knew about that fatality, and might not have approved of the uncalled-for instruction of the busybodies.

On another evening later in the year 1948, while Mother was staying at Jhusi in Sri Prabhu Dutt Brahmachari's Ashram, I went there for Her *darsan* at the invitation of certain clients of mine who were also putting up there. I sat for a while at Mother's feet without having anything to say. She put a few casual questions to my clients so as to know where they came from. As at that time of the season the pontoon bridge was being dismantled, I was in a hurry to get back across the bridge before it became dark, so I got up to take leave of Her. She directed one of Her Bhaktas to get some prasad for me. There was a moment's delay and I was getting impatient to leave. She made a sign to get the prasad quickly, not once but twice, as I was hurrying out of Her presence. A big *laddoo* (a sweet) was at last handed over to me

just as I was on the point of leaving the place, and I
carried it with me as if it were a prize won by me for
all the trouble I had taken in going as far as Jhusi to
have Mother's *darsan.* On reaching home, I found
my wife suffering from a serious attack of colic and
diarrhoea. As night advanced, her trouble grew worse
and worse, and no medicine seemed to help. At
about midnight, I felt there was no hope of saving
her life, and so I thought Mother's prasad which lay
in my pocket might possibly come to my rescue,
and with trembling hands and with Ramnama on my
lips, I forced a little bit into my wife's mouth, while
she was almost sinking. Soon *after I was happy to
notice that she had fallen asleep and that was
end of her malady.*

About two years later when it was again my good
fortune to enjoy Mother's *darsan* at the house of one
of my neighbours, it is not possible for me to describe
the effect of the few words that fell from Her august
lips in dispelling certain doubts that had arisen in my
mind. When I found She had not touched the offering
of sweets I had brought for Her, I protested to Her
why She was not accepting any of it and narrated to
Her how I had found Her prasad efficacious in saving
my wife's life. She said with Her usual smile and the
condescension of a Goddess that She had already
accepted it, and for my satisfaction She took a
particle of it and made a show of putting it into Her
mouth, Whereupon Her devotee, known as Didi,
remarked that Mataji had not a single grain of food
for the last three days.

During the last Durga Puja celebrated by Mother's
bhaktas at Allahabad, I wished I could ask Mother

to give me some of Her prasad once again. I had kept that wish all to myself, but to my great astonishment, a volunteer Bhakta approached to tell me that I should not fail to take Mother's prasad at noon the next day. Next morning I found another volunteer Bhakta comming to tell me that I should like Mother's prasad as Mother had given an express direction to carry that message to me. But for that reminder, I might not have gone to take the prasad at lunch time. I had no idea that invitation for prasad really meant an invitation for lunch. So I went to partook of a sumptuous lunch in the company of a host of Mother's Bhaktas, and for three days I had a feeling of such a purification of the body as one feels after a bath in the Gangas.

Twelve

(As narrated by Sri U.C. Dutt)

In the Spring of 1969 I went to Rajpur, Dehradun, at an invitation from a Training Institute and stayed there for a week. From Mata Anandamayee Ashram, Kishenpur, I could gather that Mother had not been at all well recently. She was taking rest at Ananda Kashi in the lap of the Himalayas. The place is thirty miles from Hardwar on the road to Deva Prayag, I did not like to miss the chance of seeing Mother in those surroundings, with the Ganga flowing through the Himalayas.

Before leaving the area, I went to Mussoorie to see my relation, Dr. J.K. Dutta, Medical Officer, St. George's College. On the Basanti Mahastami evening (4th April), Dr. Dutta and I were taking rest in silence on beds side by side, when Dr. Dutta exclaimed suddenly, "What is this? How can this be?" "What is the matter?" said I. He replied, "Ma appeared with a crown on Her head. She stood for a while. Does She wear a crown?" I told m that Ma had been given a crown on Her 60th birthday. I enquired if the crown was white. Doctor Dutta said that it was **YELLOW.** I became speechless. Our eyes were turned in the same direction of the room. The Doctor was lucky to have Mother's *darsan* in his bed-room, while I could see only the wall, door and furniture. Is it because he is more desering or was I being drawn to Her presence soon?

A few days later, I was at Ananda Kashi on April 1. It is a beauty spot; lofty green hillocks ranged in a line like sentinels overlooking the babbling streams of greenish white below; red, white, pink and yellow flowers blooming here and there in the gardens and orchards blossomed and bent. The blue vault of heaven hung overhead as the symbol of the Infinite. All the aspects of nature vied with one another to add to the sublimity of the place. Why is it called Ananda Kashi? It is named 'Kashi' as the Ganga flows north ward and 'Ananda' after the blissful Mother Anandamayee.

It was 9 o'clock in the morning when the lovely sights greeted me. Along with some known faces, I found there two Italian devotees, an old lady and a young stalwart, waiting to bid good-bye to Mother. They were leaving after a stay there of a few days. Mother would come out untimely to see them off.

I met the lady and the young man in a porch close to Mother's temple. The young man seemed to take keen interest in Yoga. He had a giant figure. Jovial by nature and friendly with all, his eyes sparkled when he saw me. After a word or two, he asked me with which mythological person I should compare him. At once I said "Bhima". He refused to accept the honour of a comparison with our Indian Hercules. He liked to be Ganesa with a long trunk and a quill pen in his hand to be a scribe to Vyasa. He desired to be accepted as one of Mother's children. He took my address and told me that I would see him shortly clad in the robe of a wanderer, moving along Indian roads.

Mother came out of Her room, sat on the verandah and by Her divine presence showered grace on all of us. She smiled as usual when She saw me and chatted humorously with the Italian guests. On taking leave, 'Ganesh' was almost in tears.

At the after-dusk sitting, which continued till 9 p.m. including the period of slience, I related to Mother Dr. Dutta's vision of Her at Mussoorie on the Mahastami night. Mother told me that She had been thinking of him on that day. She had been to his Mussoorie house once, many years ago, with Bhaiji. The Doctor's wife had prepared puris, vegetables, etc. and entertained them. In the evening, Mother came down to Rajpur on foot and felt thirsty. I do not remember now whether at that time or on some other occasion when Her throat became parched due to excessive thirst, while drinking water could not be procured, a devotee in Bengal offered water-melon to Mother as bhoga. Consequently Her thirst was appeased and the fact of the offering was duly verified by Bhaiji. *Mother thought of the Doctor and that thought took shape and appeared before him.*

Thinking and being became identical. How to explain the crown? On that very day, I was told, a lady devotee had placed a mukut (crown) of yellow flowers on Mother's head. So the vision was wearing a yellow crown.

Captain Amal Roy was with us. He is a disciple of Bala Bholanath. At one meeting, he have a vivid description of how Mother saved his life in the battle-field of Kashmir when bombs and shells were dropped by the Pakistanis. The charms of moonlit night in the 'heaven on earth' combined with a sense of duty to help the sufferers, dragged the doctor almost unconsciously out of his safe shelter to the danger zone. Having realized his position in 'the valley of death', he was going to take cover at one point when a sweet and distint *voice was heard within, saying: "Do not sit here." He knew the voice and responded to the call. He then sat down behind a boulder a few steps away. At that moment, a bomb fell and burst where he had intended to sit at first. As a result, a vaccum was created and he could not breathe for a while. However, he was saved. It was a narrow escape through Mother's grace.*

Thirteen

(As narrated by Sri K.G. Ambegaokar, I.C.S.,(Retd.)

Usually a *Bhagavata* week is arranged by some individual for a special reason like the peace of the soul of a deceased relation. This time it was held at Naimisaranya and this was one of the rare occasions when the *saptah* was arranged by the Ashram. Mataji told us later how this had happened. After the *Saptah* was performed in Varanasi some years ago, one lady had voiced the wish of several people that another Saptah should be held soon. Mataji who knew that the last one had cost a lot and another one would cost not less than Rs.25,000/—, had declined. But the lady was insistent, had put down Rs.1000/— herself and several other persons had collected about Rs.4000/—. This money remained in a Bank for 4/5 years and in the meanwhile the lady died. So this time though the money was inadequate, it was decided to celebrate the Saptah and Yogibhai, the Raja of Solan, had suggested Naimisharanya. The actual cost had run upto Rs.35,000/— but the money had somehow come!

I must relate two incidents connected with the *Bhagavata Saptah* about which we came to know subsequently.

One of the readers of the Bhagavata was Sri Pandit Vasistha Dutt Misra, a Professor in the Banaras Hindu University, who also teaches the students of the Ashram Kanyapeeth. After the reading of the Bhagavata was over on 3rd Dec., he was returning by train to Varanasi. At Balamau Station at night while trying to get water from an overhead hydrant in between the railway tracks, he was knocked down by a goods engine which ran over his right arm and cut it off just below the shoulder. Any other person would have died of shock or at least fainted, but this gentleman calmly picked up his severed arm with his left hand and walked up to the railway platform.

In the absence of any medical aid there, the Station Master arranged to send him to another station Sandila. The Railway Engineer, Sri H.C. Banerjee, one of Mataji's devotees, hearing of the accident, went to the Railway Hospital in Sandila and enquiring about the patient from the doctor-in-charge, was surprised to find Mr. Misra sitting up on a blood-stained bed with a beaming ruddy countenance and absolutely unconcerned! As the hospital was ill-equipped, it was decided to take him to Banaras. After a week or ten days, he was reported to be progressing satisfactorily. Whenever people express surprise that such a sad mishap should have occurred immediately after his participation in the Bhagavata Saptah, he cheerfully replies that his time had come to die and it was the Bhagavata reading which had saved his life at the loss of only one arm! *Mataji remarked while relating the incident that it was the Bhagavata which had made him sthitapragna (Steadfast and calm).*

Even the accident might possibly be explained by the fact that he had left without waiting for the purnahuti (completion sacrifice) next day and without taking leave from Mataji. Furthermore, according to Hindu faith, however good and godly you may be in this life (for which your reward will come in due course), you cannot escape your *prarabdha karma,* the past actions which have started bearing fruit in the present.

The second incident is not as gruesome as the first but a pleasing one that illustrates how Mataji lives the life She preaches, of recognizing God in everyone. The day after the camp was dismantled and most people had left, while we were sitting near Mataji on the verandah of Her cottage, a woman dressed in a gorgeous Banarasi sari and bedecked with ornaments, came up with a plate to do *arati* to Mataji. She was a sweeper woman of the camp to whom Ma had given away the sari and the ornaments that had been presented as an offering to Mataji at the end of the functions by one of Raja Sahebs.

Fourteen

(As recorded by Didi Gurupriya Devi in her Diary)

19 June 59. A devotee has arrived with his wife and daughter-in-law. The gentleman is a vanaprasthi (one who has abandoned his life as a householder in order to devote the rest of his days entirely to the search after God or Truth) and his daughter-in-law also intends to take up the same kind of life. She seems to be in some special state; her father-in-law at least praises her a lot. He says that their Guru, who lives in Varanasi, has on seeing her declared that her condition was a highly spiritual one. He sought Mataji's opinion about it.

Mataji asked the young woman: "What do you experience while meditating?" "At first I feel intense bliss and at the end again," she replied, "but in between nothing at all."

Mataji commented: "This is still an elementary stage. You can understand it for yourself: as long as the ego-mind persists, there can be no samadhi. Nevertheless, her mind and body may be said to have attained to a certain degree of stillness. Her own words give the clue: 'at first there is bliss, then nothing at all' — who is the experiencer of all this? So long as the individual mind is active, there is no samadhi."

After a pause Mataji continued: "Someone else also came to this body, declaring that he was no longer interested in any work or occupation; since his mind got absorbed in samadhi and that his Kundalini had been aroused. While speaking, he frequently used the words 'I' and 'mine'. He was given to understand that there could be no question of samadhi so long as there was 'I' or 'mine'. In real samadhi, none of this survives. Look, a mango when ripe on a tree does not call out: 'I am ripe, come and take me.' Do you see the beauty of it? It returns to the very place from which it had originated."

The gentleman seemed extremely pleased with what Mataji had said. She then introduced the big girls of the Ashram to him with the words: "They all are my friends; they come from good families and are well educated. Some have passed their M.A., B.A., etc., yet renouncing everything, they have gathered round this body to tread this path. This body does not know how to serve anyone; all the same, my friends in their kindness have great affection for this little child."

The gentleman then expressed his wish to leave his daughter-in-law in Mataji's charge, informing her that she comes of a well-to-do family. At first she seemed to be full of enthusiasm, but on hearing all that Mataji had said, a change had obviously come over her.

Mataji further remarked: "It is not always possible to keep the girls with me. They live a somewhat secluded life. Friend, this path is very difficult. Everyone who comes has a different up-bringing and a different way of looking at things. All this had to be ignored. Whoever blames or reproaches one, has actually contributed thereby to one's spiritual progress."

20 June 59. — Today the gentleman left together with his wife. Mataji asked the daughter-in-law: "You won't cry at the parting, will you?"

In the evening, Dr. Gopinath Kaviraj left for Kashi. Mataji went by car to see him off at the station. The gentleman and his wife also were travelling by the same train. So we met them once more at the railway platform. Their daughter-in-law also had come with Mataji. On seeing her, the gentleman exclaimed full of enthusiasm: "Mataji, has the girl already passed her test? You yourself seemed doubtful as to whether she would be able to bear Ashram life."

Mataji smiled. "It is the final test that alone counts," was her laconic reply.

22 June 59 — Yesterday two telegrams were received from the girl's husband, requesting her to return home without delay. Since then, she is feeling restless. Early morning, her father-in-law turned up in person to take her home. Many who had witnessed the whole incident were greatly surprised at his sudden return. But Mataji knows everything; already much earlier she had remarked: "Wait and see what will be the final outcome of it all. In the end, the truth must come to light, whatever it may be. Never

prevent people from having their own way." As regards the telegrams, Mataji told the gentleman: "Father, if during those three or three and a half years your son had not enjoyed his married life fully, he would not have been so impatient to have his wife back."

At long last, the gentleman had come to understand the meaning of all that Mataji had said. That very day he departed with his daughter-in-law.

Fifteen
(As narrated by Br. Vijaiananda)

We have frequently heard Mother say that She does not go anywhere; yet we see Her travel from place to place. Being all-prevading and therefore everywhere at all times, Her body and its movements have significance only for us. Mother has assured us that She will never leave us, no matter where we may go or what we may do. I feel convinced that She is the all-pervading Divine Consciousness, for whom there is no limitation of space and time, for whom the word 'impossible' has no meaning. However, for most of us, this knowledge is only on the level of the spoken word. Many just repeat it from hearsay. But those who have for a longer period of time lived under Mother's guidance, have experienced in a variety of ways the benediction of Her presence, and are able to understand that Her blessings and Her divine love are the same, whether we are far or near Her physically. But our mind is like a stupid child that has to be taught his lesson again and again, because he keeps on forgetting it, until it is hammered right into his brain. On occasions, something happens that impresses deeply on our foolish minds the evident fact that Mother is ever   with us, seated in our own hearts, guiding us constantly, removing obstacles, saving us from dangers. It is to this that I want to refer here, of two incidents.

1

In 1954, Mother's birthday celebrations took place in the Almora Ashram. I was then staying at the Varanasi Ashram and from there proceeded to Almora to attend the function. Already for three years, I had enjoyed the good fortune of living under Mother's direct guidance. During the first half of this period, I had constantly travelled with Mother, accompanying Her wherever She would go. To leave Her even for a single day was a source of almost unbearable mental suffering to me. This is how Mother at first attracts us towards Her physical presence, in order to wean our minds from all worldly attachment. Love for Mother purifies mind and heart, awakens and greatly increases our yearning for the Divine. What may be achieved after long years of struggle by the practices of pranayama, japa, or self-inquiry, is accomplished within a short period of time, effortlessly as it were, by pure and intense love for Mother. In fact, intense pure and selfless love for Mother is in itself a most powerful sadhana. This love has then to be expanded progressively to the all-pervading presence. Thus Mother leads us stage by stage.

Some temperaments may actually feel Mother nearer while they are far away from Her in space.

This may sound paradoxical, but can be explained as follows: When we are with Mother physically, Her sweetness and kindness, Her childlike simplicity may make us at times forget Her divinity. While far away, if the mind is capable of rising beyond the physical aspect, we have perhaps a greater chance of grasping that which abides in the heart.

But let me again take up the thread of my story. During the second half of the three years that I had spent travelling with Mother, I could bear to remain without Her for short intervals; but never (as far as I remember) had I been without Mother's *darsan* for more than a month. When I came to Almora for the birthday celebrations, the yearning for Mother's physical presence had come again, even stronger than before. The infinite love of the Guru is quite different from what is usually called 'love'. Real Love knows no weakness. It may even appear hard and merciless on occasions. The grown-up child was clinging to the toys of the baby, and Mother most probably knew that the time had come for him to shake off the habits of the infant. Mother's skill in seizing the psychological moment is well-known. At such a moment, I was made to promise to remain in the Almora Ashram for one whole year, without travelling anywhere. One whole year without seeing Mother! It seemed like eternity to me. Previously, even after fifteen days of separation, I would count the days and wait for Mother's return, like the well-known chatak bird for the rain.

Mother stayed for more than two months at Almora that summer. Whilst She was there, a number of improvements were made in the Ashram. Only too soon the inevitable day of Mother's departure came. I was standing by the road-side, looking at Mother's car that was ready to start. It was beyond my imagination that Mother, knowing my state of mind, could leave me behind for such a long period. *Before starting, She called me, gave me Her blessing and uttered a few kind and soothing words.* The car began to speed down the road to Kathgodam. I followed it with my eyes until it vanished out of sight. All kinds of childish ideas flashed through my mind. I thought that Mother was just testing me and soon would send back someone with a message for me to join Her. But the time passed and nobody came. My mind was overcast by sadn   as the sky by dark clouds. I felt helplessly desp   dent and depressed. Of course, I was not compelled to stay on. (I have never witnessed Mother exercising compulsion over anyone). I could have easily followed Mother to the plains — She would probably have laughed the matter over, as had in fact happened on a former occasion, and waited for a better opportunity to make me stay in solitude. But then I had given my word and, moreover, my mind having matured in the meanwhile, I understood that it was necessary for me to practise sadhana and lead a secluded life. I thus tried to divert my thoughts from their painful one-pointedness, keeping myself engaged in some work or other. During Mother's sojourn at Almora, I had temporarily occupied a room near the tank of the Patal Devi temple, since the Ashram had been overcrowded. Now I had to shift to the Ashram. So I began to pack and arrange my belongings. But my sorrow would not leave me. I was slowly

ascending the narrow path leading from Patal Devi
to the Ashram. The sky was spotlessly blue, the air
fresh and light. In the plains, I mused, there must be
broiling heat, heavy with dampness. Here at Almora
was the calm stillness of the Himalayan mountains
with their sublime beauty. In the plains, I would
have been in the midst of the din and bustle of the
towns. Travelling with Mother means enduring all
kinds of hardships and inconveniences. Here I had
every facility, as if I were in my own home. But of
what value were the beautiful scenes, the bracing
climate, the physical comforts and all the rest, when
the main thing was lacking, namely, the happiness I
found in Mother's presence! It was a happiness that
did not depend on any outer circumstance.

With eyes veiled by tears, I was gazing at the
gorgeous range of mountain peaks. *All of a sudden,*
something extraordinary happened. My whole being
was flooded with joy. Mother was there! Here,
present before me! Yet, not in Her physical form .....
But how to describe what cannot be put into words?
There was no form — Yet I could clearly see Her
long black hair floating along the mountain ridges.
There was no face, although I could distinctly per-
ceive Her divinely sweet smile filling my heart with
inexpressible joy and peace. Glued to the spot, I
stood like a small child gazing in awe and wonder at
Her majestic features. She was outside and also inside
of me — verily She was my life-force, my prana
having taken shape. No sound could be heard, but in
the depths of my heart I understood the meaning of
Her silence. It was telling me: "Why do you lament,
O fool? I have not gone far away from you; I am ever

with you, ever present in your heart, I am your Real Self." This experience lasted for a few minutes only, but it sufficed to disperse the clouds of my misery, to chase away the heavy mists that had obscured my understanding.

2

Not only in times of distress is Mother present; She is ever watchful, even where the small details of our daily routine are concerned. The following is an instance of how we are sometimes made aware of this fact.

It happened at the Varanasi Ashram. At the time to which my story refers, some threatening cracks had already appeared in the hall below the terrace protruding over the Ganges. The hall could not anymore be used for public gatherings, and visitors were not allowed to go downstairs. Only a few inmates occupied some of the side rooms. I happened to be one of those fortunate ones. I say 'fortunate', for I enjoyed the great privilege of living in solitude, right in the midst of that crowded Ashram. My room, facing the Ganges, was near "Anandamayee Ghat". In the stillness of night, I frequently would sit in the hall near a window that opened out unto the river.

Next to the Ashram, on top of the ghat is a small shrine, dedicated to Sri Ganesa. Every year the community of fishermen who live in the vicinity, organize a function that continues for five days. On this occasion, a raised platform is erected over the ghat. A canvas roof and canvas walls are pitched over the platform and beautifully decorated. Every evening, when their day's work is over, the devotees assemble in the pandal where kirtan, devotional singing and the recitation of scriptures continue until late at night.

During one of those nights, I was as usual sitting in the hall looking down at the river. Mother was not at Varanasi at that time. I could distinctly hear all that was being said or sung at the function on the ghat. Frequently, sadhakas of the Ashram who keep themselves engaged in regular spiritual practice and live a secluded life, become very sensitive to the noise and vibrations of their surroundings. This was also the case with me at that time. But the loudness of the function did not disturb me at all, so long as it was of a religious nature. On the contrary, I listened with great joy and appreciation to the Nama kirtan and the bhajans. But all other kinds of sound or noise would sometimes considerably upset me.

That night I could observe that the mood of the people on the platform was gradually changing. Although I was unable to understand the words of their songs, yet the tunes and the laughter of the audience gave me the impression that the celebrations had taken a worldly turn. It was perhaps quite harmless and, moreover, my impression might have been wrong; but that night I seemed particularly sensitive and felt quite disturbed. In a prayerful mood, I said mentally,: "In holy Kashi, on the banks of the Ganga, next to Sri Ma Anandamayee Ashram, how can one possibly indulge in vulgar songs? They should at least sing the Mahamantra!"

No sooner had this prayer taken shape in my mind than I heard a mighty sound — I could even say that

I 'saw' the sound. It is a well-known fact that sound and form are intimately connected. There is a level of perception where the two mingle. *The sound I heard was not uttered by any human voice, it had its own living personality. It came like a huge wave from the terrace of the Ashram, flowing down into the hall and finally enveloping the platform below where the function was in progress. Although the wave had no definite shape, I somehow felt that it was connected with Mother's physical presence. The sound-wave uttered once only "Hari Bol"* (which means "repeat the name of the Lord"), *but not in the tune in which Mother usually sings these words. Here the voice was mighty and stern, like a rebuke or severe command. No sooner had the wave engulf-ed the platform, than the people present stopped singing instantaneously. A blank silence prevailed for a few minutes. Then, without any transition, they began to chant: "Hare Ram, Hare Ram, Ram, Ram, Hare, Hare",* which is the second verse of the Mahamantra. They continued with this for some time, without singing the first verse (Hare Krishna etc.). Later they sang "Sitaram, Sitaram" and, as far as I remember, the remaining part of the night was spent in singing Nam Kirtan.

My prayer was a childish one and hardly deserved such a supernatural response. But very likely it was one of those psychological moments, a moment of conjunction, brought about by the interplay of various factors, in which the lesson, so frequently forgotten, could be hammered into the mind of the above-mentioned child.

Sixteen

(As recorded by Didi Gurupriya Devi in her Diary)

7 July 59 — This morning, in the course of some conversation, Mataji disclosed that She had on a subtle plane seen Swami Sankarananda of Kashi, who came to Her and said, "Ma, I am shifting to another house," On hearing this, Ma felt rather concerned, fearing that something might have happened to the Swami.

In the evening, **Choudhry Shersingh's daughter,** Darsan Kumari, came with her son Ravi to see Mataji. Ravi had recently been very seriously ill at Lucknow. We had repeatedly received news about his most precarious condition. His mother, with her eyes full of tears related the whole story of his illness to Mataji. A short time ago, he was hovering between life and death. His temperature shot up to 107°. His body seemed to be suffused with poison 'and the doctors wrapped him into ice. *Suddenly Ravi felt as if the breath was leaving his body. At that very instant, he remembered Anandamayee Ma, and in the midst of his delirium, he screamed "Ma, Ma!" No sooner had he uttered the cry, then it seemed to him that he commanded sufficient strength and vigour, that Ma Anandamayi was with him, and that there was nothing to be afraid of. Slowly the patient recovered.*

Some time before he fell ill, his mother had come to the Ashram with him. Ravi's character was not quite flawless. This is why his mother had on various occasions prayed to Mataji that he might be freed from all his weaknesses. Accordingly, Mataji had

repeatedly told Ravi, "Give up all these bad habits.
They will only drag you deeper and deeper into that
which is death."

The astonishing thing is that, during Ravi's illness,
the doctors declared that unless he gave up alcohol
for the rest of his days, the hopes of saving his life
were extremely meagre. Ravi was therefore frighten-
ed and, besides, his mother reminded him again and
again of the fact that he owed his life only to Mataji's
unbounded mercy. His family were firmly convinced
that Ravi's recovery was solely due to Mataji's
Khayal.

10 July 59.   At night, Mataji came and sat in my
room. Pandit Sunderlal and a number of others were
present. The Pandit asked Mataji: "When Bhaiji was
about to drown in the Ganges, while you were far
away, and you suddenly appeared and rescued him,
did you go there in your physical body? For the
strange thing was that at that exact time, your clothes
were dripping wet, as everyone present could see.;"
Mataji: "Pitaji, anything is possible. All bodies are in
fact my bodies. Here itself is Kashi, the Ganges —
everything. Therefore even from here, everything
may take place. Anything may happen to this body.
That its clothes were drenched on that occasion is a
clear and simple illustration of this fact."

13 March 57.   Mataji is at Vrindaban. This morning, Sri Bhaktaraja Maharaj, an old sadhu of the
Ramakrisna Mission, came for Her *darshan*. He
talked to Mataji for quite a long time. Before leaving,
he bowed down, touching the ground with his forehead, and said to the assembled people: *"This time,*

*he has come in the shape of a woman. In Her body,
everyone should recognize his own Ista. Our connection with Mataji has not been newly established, it
has existed from birth to birt , throughout eternity."*

Today a woman, named Kasturi Devi, came for
Mataji's *darshan.* She is a disciple of Sri Kishori Das
Babaji of Vrindaban. She related something most
interesting.

One night she was crying in her desperate yearning
to win the Lord's Grace. None of her attempts at
Sadhana had brought the desired result. Later in the
night she dreamt of a woman dressed all in white,
who was accompanied by a girl wearing the ochre
robe. The girl took Kasturi's hand and said, "Why
do you cry? Your Lord is here itself. Come with me,
quick!"

She dreamt the same kind of dream on two successive nights. A few days ago, she heard someone say
that there was a DEVI at Vrindaban, called "Sri
Anandamayi Ma." Thus she had come for Mataji's
darshan today. Udas (one of Mataji's attendants)
was sitting near Mataji. On seeing her, Kasturi was
struck with amazement, as she recognized in her the
girl dressed in ochre of whom she had dreamt for
two successive nights. *When she thereupon scrutiniz-
ed Mataji's face, she at once realized that the woman
in white whom she had seen in her dreams was the
exact likeness of Mataji.*

Seventeen
(As narrated by Sri Krishnanatha)

It seems appropriate to mention some of the anecdotes from Mataji's life, which She Herself related from time to time when reminded; some of these have a miraculous quality, but Mataji told them as if they were ordinary happenings.

Once a young woman of about 20 or 22 asked for Ma's help in her devotional practices. As there was a large crowd at the time, Mataji told her to see Her in private afterwards, but she did not get a chance to talk to Her. After a few days, the girl came and said that Mataji had appeared to her in a dream and whispered a Mantra into her ear. SHE repeated it and it was in pure Sanskrit though the girl was illiterate.

It then transpired that when the girl dreamt, Mataji was thinking of her. Mataji asked her not to eat meat in the months of Baisakh, Sravan, Kartick and Magh. The girl said she had already given up eating meat, though everyone else in her home take it.

At another place, Mataji said to a very dark girl of 12 or 13 who came to see Her once, "You want the necklace, don't you?" and asked Udas to bring it. When it was brought and given to the girl, everyone was surprised to see that it was a string of very valuable pearls, which had been presented to Mataji a few days earlier by the Rani of Sirmur! On that day, when Mataji was wearing the pearls on Her wrist, She had seen this little girl in the crowd, whispering to her mother that she wanted them. *Mataji wanted to give them to the girl at that very time, but she had disappeared. Mataji knew that she would come after a few days and had told Udas to keep the string with her and to bring it whenever Mataji would ask for it; that is how the pearl necklace was brought and given to the girl.*

Later on the girl had come again to show how nice the white pearls looked against her dark skin. Mataji said that when She was living in Ashtagram, there used to be low-caste people dwelling near by, and a little girl of theirs used to come and stand at a distance looking at Her. This was about 40 years ago. The little girl who got the necklace was the *same low-caste girl in a previous birth.*

Mataji's habit of giving away whatever valuable presents She receives is well-known. It has already been related previously how a costly Benarasi sari and ornaments, received at the end of a Bhagavat *Saptah,* were bestowed on a sweeper woman. As for smaller gifts like sweets, fruits, flowers or garlands, they are given away immediately. Referring to this, Mataji once humourously remarked that She noticed how the face of the donor becomes smaller and smaller as She started distributing his offering. Dr. Pannalal told us two stories in this connection. Once some students had brought an expensive garland for Her and as usual She immediately gave it away. The students said, 'we wished, you had worn it at least for ten minutes to please us.' Mataji replied: *"If I am to wear it for ten minutes to please you, will you do whatever I tell you to please me?"* There was dead silence — nobody dared to say 'yes' for fear that She might ask them something they would not be able to fulfil.

On another occasion, when Mataji was going away
by train, Dr. Pannalal had brought for Her some
oranges and told Gurupriya Didi to keep them hidden
under the berth till the train started, so that Mataji
might not give them away. Mataji was not told
anything about this, but just as the train began to
move She put Her hand under the berth, took out
the oranges and started throwing them to the people
on the platform. Those who often go for Mataji's
darshan are familiar with Her way of throwing fruits
and other things into the crowd for people to catch,
and they know how good She is at it.

*   *   *

We learnt one day from Gurupriya Didi that
Mataji's munificence had earned for Her in Naimisaranya the reputation of being the Goddess of Wealth
incarnate. A lady who arrived at the camp that day
had heard the coolies at the railway station say that
a Mataji had come who was an Avatar of Laxmi
She gives away gold thrones and ashrafies (gold
coins)! Mataji laughed when She heard this and told
us that for the *Bhagavat Saptah,* She had enquired
what was prescribed in the Scriptures to be given as
Dan (gift). On hearing that it was 12 tolas of gold,
She had asked one fourth of it, i.e., 3 tolas to be used
to give a gold polish to a silver throne on which the
sacred book was to be placed for reading. This was
given away to the purohit (priest) at the end, and
people thought it was a gold throne. I forgot what
Ma said about another three tolas of gold, but the
remainder was given away in the form of a gold

ashrafi to each of the 108 readers. No wonder Mataji seemed Laxmi incarnate to poor people who had never seen so much gold being distributed.

*   *   *

In the course of his discourse on the Narada Bhaktisutra, Dr. Pannalal was once talking about how great saints come to the help of their devotees, and in this connection, he related two stories about Mataji. She had once gone in a boat to the other bank of the Ganges and a devotee on this side wanted to join Her. He jumped into the river and started to swim across, but when he had reached half way, began to drown. There was no one to rescue him and so he cried out to Ma. Suddenly, apparently from nowhere, a boat appeared and saved him. On another occasion, Ma's great devotee, Bhaiji, while drowning in Benaras, was pulled out by an old woman who waded into the river. *At that time, Ma was actually in Dehradun and those near Her saw, to their surprise that Her clothes were dripping wet.*

*   *   *

Another story was told by Mataji Herself about how one of Her devotees had once made up his mind to die at Her feet and for this purpose had taken a very large dose of opium and eaten sweets thereafter to make the poison more deadly. When he was quite sure he could not be saved, he came and lay clinging to Mataji's feet. Even though nobody was aware at the time that he had taken poison,

Mataji somehow kept him awake through the rest of the night. In the morning, there were all sorts of difficulties in transporting him to the hospital and getting medical aid, but these were somehow surmounted and he was saved against all odds.

Eighteen
(As recorded by Didi Gurupriya Devi in her Diary)

20 July 57 — A gentleman aged 84, who had recently lost his son, cried and lamented a great deal over his bereavement. Sitting near Mataji for some time, he became much calmer. In this connection, Mataji related something that had happened many years ago, while She was at Tarapith:

A woman came to Mataji in deep sorrow. Her eldest daughter had died suddenly, just at the time when all the preparations for her wedding had been completed. The woman brought her younger daughter with her who was then about 11 years old. When Mataji visited Tarapith again the next year, the woman gave Her the sad news that her younger daughter had also passed away. God's will is inscrutable. It so happened that Mataji came to Tarapith once again a year later. This time the same woman was carrying a baby, a month old, in her arms when she came for Mataji's *darsan*. The woman related to Mataji in detail what had happened in the mean time.

After her younger daughter had left this world, the bereaved mother was simply heart-broken and could not stop crying. One night she dreamt of her

younger girl. She saw her in a most lovely place,
together with many other children of her age. They
all looked happy and seemed to be engaged in praying
to God. A few days later, the child's father dreamt
that his younger daughter came to him and told to
him full of grief that she could not remain in her
charming abode any longer since she was unable to
bear her mother's deep sorrow for her. She would
therefore return to her. In his dream, the 11 years
old girl suddenly changed into a tiny infant, which
he placed into his wife's lap. Lo and behold, within a
year a baby girl was born to them. This was the child
that she had now brought with her to Mataji.

Mataji commented on this story as follows: "To
weep and lament over the loss of a loved person, at
times interferes with the spiritual progress of the
deceased. One comes across other stories of a similar
kind. It is man's duty to remain steady and calm
under all circumstances, and to pray only for the
welfare of the soul (atma)".

I have heard another story from Mataji that may
be repeated here: A certain pandit was very friendly
with a fakir. One day the pandit smelt a distinct
scent of ripe jack-fruit, although it was not the season
for it. He searched everywhere, trying to locate the
source of the fragrance, without any result whatever.
He felt extremely puzzled and finally went to his
friend, the fakir, to solicit his opinion on the strange
sensation. The fakir was somewhat advanced on the
spiritual path and had acquired some supernormal
powers. He listened to all that the pandit told him
and then sat in silence for a while. Thereupon he
asked his friend to accompany him. They walked

some distance, crossed a river, and again walked until they came to a village. There they found an old Brahmin performing Sraddha (a ceremony performed for the dead) for his father. In order to satisfy the soul of the deceased, he had offered ripe jack-fruit during the ceremony. His father had been specially fond of jack-fruit and therefore the Brahmin had taken the trouble to procure some of it, although it was out of season in that part of the country. The fakir explained to his friend: "Look, in your last birth you were the father of this Brahmin. When he offered jack-fruit to you in the course of the ritual the scent of the fruit floated to you, although you were far away, sitting in your own house."

Whether this story is true or not is difficult to say. Somebody had once related it to Mataji. After narrating the story, Mataji said: "Whatever is offered to a deceased person in the sraddha ceremony, reaches him in some manner and gives him satisfaction. Nowadays one often hears people question whether the sraddha really benefits the dead and in what way. In actual fact, there are many true stories of a more or less similar type that can establish your faith in the matter. One should not make light of anything."

*   *   *

2 Aug. 57 — Yesterday afternoon, Mrs. Sabharwal with her son and daughter-in-law came to see Mataji. The young couple are about to go to England and have come to seek Mataji's blessing. Before they took leave of Her, Mataji gave two fruits to the young woman. Mrs. Sabharwal exclaimed with

amusement: "Again these fruits, Mataji!" We at first could not quite understand what was meant by this remark. Later we heard that she was referring to something that had happened many years ago. It was like this:

A Kashmere devotee, who was then working in the Police Department in U.P., had come to Kishenpur with his wife for Mataji's *darsan* on his way down from Mussoorie. On taking leave, Mataji put three fruits into his wife's hands. Why three, Mataji alone knew. They had so far been childless. The surprising thing was that after partaking of those fruits, three children were born to them, one after another. They felt convinced that the births of their children were due solely to Mataji's grace. However, they never breathed a word about this to Mataji. Years later, when the gentleman had become a high police official in Lucknow, Mataji once visited that town. The husband and the wife came for Mataji's darshan. When Mataji wanted to present two fruits to the lady, she folded her hands saying: "We don't want any more children." On that occasion, they explained to Mataji why she would not accept the fruits! The other day the same lady came for Mataji's *darsan* and referred to the above-mentioned incident while sitting in Mataji's room in Mrs. Sabharwal's presence. Thus when yesterday Mataji presented two fruits to Mrs. Sabharwal's daughter-in-law, she took it to mean that two children would be born to her. So many presents does Mataji give constantly to people! The actual fact is that according to their Heart's desire, people address prayers to Mataji mentally and what they see as a result depends on their desires.

Now let me refer to another incident that took place some years ago. One day Mataji was leaving Banaras for some other place. On her way to the railway station, She stopped the car in front of Dr. G.Das Gupta's house. The whole family came out to receive Her. When the youngest daughter Radhu bowed to Mataji, She ·gave her two garlands of flowers. Those who witnessed this wondered why Radhu had received two garlands.

A short time later, when Mataji was in Bombay, a letter arrived from Dr. G. Das Gupta to inform her that he had quite unexpectedly found a suitable bridegroom for Radhu and thus arranged for her marriage. At the time when Mataji had given two garlands to Radhu, nobody was as yet thinking of her marriage. But Mataji, who is all-knowing, had already given her a garland for herself and another for her future husband. Similar things happen daily with Mataji. How few are the miracles we notice!

*   *   *

13 April 62 — In the afternoon, Mataji suddenly walked out of the Kankhal Ashram compound, crossed the road and proceeded straight to the Ganges. A large group of Ashramites and visitors followed Her. Everyone was asked to sit on the steps leading to the Ganges. A ceremony was in progress at the neighbouring burning-ghat. We saw military and police march in formation, saluting the blazing funeral pyre. One of the leading officers of the Bharat Seva Sangha, who were doing devoted and very efficient service throughout the Kumbha Mela,died

of heart failure while on duty. The deceased had probably never even had Mataji's darshan during his life time, but Mataji obviously had the kheyal to give Her blessing while his body was being consumed by the flames. It was a significant and deeply moving incident. Everyone was conscious of the hush that descended on the whole assembly.

All traffic has been suspended for the whole day and night to give a chance to the pedestrians who streamed to and from the Ganges in thousands. However, at 9 p.m. some police officers came and offered to take Mataji by car to Brahmakunda. Mataji consented, although She did not descend the steps down to the river but watched the bathing pilgrims from the top. The whole day was certainly unforgettable.

Nineteen
(An incident during Samyam Saptah Mahabrata at Ahmedabad)

All arrangements were excellent and carefully thought out to the minutest detail for the *Samyam Saptah*. A dainty and artistically decorated little house built of asbestos and matting for Mataji's personal use and a large and elegant *pandal* equipped with fans, lights and loud-speakers were erected in the compound of the house where the Munshaw family lived. Many devotees, who have made it a point to take part in the Samyam Vrata every year without fail, had come from considerable distances and the bhaktas of Bombay and Gujarat naturally attended in large numbers. Among the *vratis* were also two Western guests who had come to India for the sole purpose of spending some time with Mataji.

The hardships and inconveniences of camp life that the vratis had to put up with on former occasions in places like Naimisaranya, Sukhtal, Risikesa and so forth, were this time conspicuous by their absence. The vratis were accommodated in private houses in the neighbourhood and those who stayed at a distance of half a mile or more were regularly taken backwards and forwards by cars. As if to make up for this lack of austerity, *a quite untimely and very severe thunder storm broke out on the third day of the function, just a few minutes after the collective morning meditation had started.* Torrential rain began to batter the canvas roof of the pandal and, where it gathered, it burst through the canvas with the vehemence of waterfalls. The fury of the storm seemed to threaten most of all the platform on which Mataji and the Mahatmas had their seats. A large piece of waterproof had to be held above Mataji's head by two tall men to protect Her from the water leaking through the roof and, when after a little while the roof was in danger of falling right down over head, a large rafter was brought to support the canvas. Big vessels arrived from the kitchen to catch the rain that had began to form little pools in several places of the pandal, but the vessels filled up in no time and had to be emptied again and again with the help of buckets. All this activity was carried on in complete silence. Mataji herself sat like a statue until the meditation hour was over. Many vratis followed Her example and remained in their places without budging, continuing their japa and dhyana, notwithstanding their drenched clothes. Others were forced to move from their seats and to stand up, but perfect calm and quiet was maintained by everyone. Sixteen ceiling fans and many tube-lights had been fixed in the roof of the tent and one can easily imagine what might have happened if even a part of the roof had collapsed and crashed down on the vratis. When the short *kirtan* that always follows the meditation had been sung, the announcer requested the congregation to vacate the pandal immediately, as Mataji would not leave the tent until the last person was safely seen off. As soon as the last vrati left the pandal and Mataji also came out, the huge pandal collapsed in the twinkling of an eye. It was indeed a miracle that no one was hurt. One could not help remembering the legend in which Sri Krishna is supposed to have held Mount Govardhana over the cowherds to protect them from torrential rains. Here also it seemed obvious that only Divine Grace of Mother was responsible for saving the situation.

The *vratis* were then asked to collect on the verandah and in the spacious drawing-room of the house, while Mataji who never enters the house of a grihastha, sat under the porch. The programme proceeded as scheduled without any interruption at all. In the evening, it was informed that a new pandal was under construction and would be ready in the morning. The pandal was actually ready for use the next morning with lights, fans and loud-speakers, and Mataji arrived punctually at that early hour and stayed throughout the kirtan, blessing the newly built structure with Her presence.

Thus, what might ordinarily have resulted in panic and caused even a serious calamity, became on the other hand a source of inspiration. The whole incident seemed to have been turned into an object lesson of how difficulties and emergencies should be met. A sadhaka must regard every difficulty or trouble as an opportunity to develop initiative, courage and power, as an incentive to make him proceed on his chosen path with even greater determination and vigour.

*   *   *

Twenty

During Mataji's stay in Dehradun in Aug 1964, a group of 30 body-scouts from Jullundur arrived one day. They had quite a long discussion with Mataji, who called them her friends and enjoined on them to cultivate the habit of daily remembrance of God. Some of them seemed keenly interested and asked for details about meditation. After a trip to Mussoorie, they came to say good-bye to her. When Mataji got up to retire to her room, they began to repeat in chorus like a slogan: "Ma Jullundur aao, Ma Jullundur aao" (Ma, come to Jullundur). Ma could be heard saying, "Ma is in Jullundur and Ma is travelling with you to Jullundur."

Twentyone

One morning, in the month of Oct.'64 while Mataji was in Dehradun, a European lady from Michigan arrived for her *darsan*. She was probably a journalist. She had reached Delhi only the day before by plane, took the night train to Dehradun and wanted to leave again by the afternoon bus. With considerable

impatience, she waited for Mataji to emerge from
Her room. As soon as Mataji came out, the lady at
once got busy with her camera and took photos
from all sides. She was later granted a short interview.
"When are you coming to America?" was one of the
questions put to Mataji.

"This little child is in America. Try to see her
there," was the answer. The visitor, highly pleased
with Mataji's reply, promised to follow Her advice.
She also took Mataji's assurance that 'She was always
with her', verbally in a material sense, for when someone asked her whether she intended to come again,
she promptly said: "There is no need, since Mataji is
always with me."

*   *   *

The other incident, during the same period, was
the visit of a group of ten persons from Paris, who
had come on a pilgrimage to India's holy places,
guided by their South Indian Guru who teaches
Hatha Yoga in France. They had travelled for two
nights in order to have Mataji's *darsan* and were
leaving Dehradun the same night. In the morning,
they accompanied Mataji to Kalyanvan where she
sat in the hall with them for quite some time. All
were amazed to see them doing pranama to Mataji
in the Indian way with sincere and deep reverence.
They were eager to take with them not only photo-
graphs of Mataji, but especially of Her feet! At 5
p.m., Mataji received them again, this time in Her
own room. They sat in complete silence for about 50
minutes. Fourteen Europeans and a few Ashramites

were present. The French pilgrims, who hardly knew any English, were visibly profoundly moved. On taking leave, some wished to express their gratitude to Mataji, but she interrupted: "One thanks another, not one's own self." When after a pause she added: "On the contrary, this little child must thank you for having come from such a great distance to give *darsan* to Her," many of them had tears in their eyes. They declared that, although they had had no talk with Mataji, all their questions had been answered in silence.

Twentytwo

One day, a small locket was found just outside Mataji's house. The opinions were divided as to whether the picture it contained was of Siva or Krishna. Mataji said, "When you find the owner, bring him or her to me." The locket belonged to the servant girl named Ganga, aged about 10, who had come with a lady from Agra who was staying at the Manav Seva Sangha next door and came daily for Mataji's *darsan*. Ganga had been sad and cried because she had not been allowed with her to the Ashram, but ordered to remain outside from where she secretly peeped into the room, eager to catch a glimpse of Mataji. Thus, when taken into Mataji's room, she was naturally beside herself with joy, but felt extremely shy. Mataji talked to her very sweetly, calling her 'friend' and asking her a number of questions. "Have you studied anything?" Mataji said. Ganga had to answer, "No", to which Mataji exclaimed laughingly "Then we are equals; this friend of yours has not studied anything either." Ganga's mistress later remarked that, although she did so much puja and tried her utmost to please Mataji, yet Mataji took no notice of her, while her illiterate servant girl had found favour in Mataji's eyes. Didi explained, "The person who makes preparations for the puja and scrubs the vessels is also rewarded with the fruit of worship."

*   *   *

Words of Ma

When the mind is full of worldly desires, it is their very nature to make the mind confused. This is why effort is necessary. So long as you do not become absorbed in dhyana and japa, it has to be performed by constant endeavour. To be moderate in eating, sleeping, and the like is imperative. Look, when you go on a journey, you take with you only as much as you need. You don't carry along all that is in your home. Thus, when becoming a pilgrim on the path to God, you should take only as much food and supply as will help you to live always in the presence of God. There is a saying: 'As one eats, so one becomes.' Thus, withdraw the mind from outer things and make it turn within.

*   *   *

Chapter 7

AN INCIDENT OF MOTHER'S SUPER-
NATURAL GLORY

It was summer of 1960 and I was at that time in
Bombay while Mother, to our knowledge, was in
Dehradun. One day a friend of mine came to visit
me. During our conversation, she told me that her
mother had a dream to get a small idol of Gopal
(the name of child Sri Krishna) and keep it for daily
puja. A few days later, her mother herself gave me
the details of the dream, "A relation of mine, a few
days ago, appeared in the dream and advised me to
get an idol of Gopal and worship it daily. Having
said this she disappeared. After her departure, I
saw Anandamayi Ma sitting in the verandah of
Amba Devi Temple. As I approached her, Mother
said, 'Get an idol of Gopal from this temple and
worship it.' A few days earlier, I had another dream
in which I saw a small child of dark colour playing
in front of my house and Mother was standing
nearby."

A month later, on a Sunday morning I went to
my friend's house and we planned to go out in the
evening in search of an idol of Gopal. It was however decided not to purchase an idol from the
market but to try to get one from one of the local
temples.

There are two very famous temples in Bombay —
Mahalaksmi Temple and Amba Devi Temple. We

set out that evening for Amba Devi temple. On reaching there, we found that most of the visitors were Gujaratis. We went round the main temple, and on coming out of the temple compound, found another temple. We went inside and were surprised to find many idols of Gopalji, all of different sizes. My friend met the pujari (priest) and after narrating the dream her mother had about getting an idol of Gopal, she requested him to give her a Gopal-idol. The priest thought over the proposal for a while and then said, "Normally we do not give any idol kept here to anybody, but I can give you one to worship for a few days only. However, you may come next Wednesday and we will see what can be done."

On the evening of the appointed day, we all went to Amba Devi temple, and as we entered the temple compound at about 7 p.m., we were surprised and thrilled to find none other than Sri Anandamayi Ma sitting in the verandah of the temple, surrounded by a few devotees, among whom was a Sannyasini resembling Didima who was sitting just by the side of Ma with an idol of Gopal on her lap.

For me, it was quite difficult to believe my eyes, for to find Ma at that time sitting in the verandah of Amba Devi temple in Bombay was not only un-expected but also unbelievable, as, according to my latest information, Ma was on that day and time in Dehradun. My mind was agitated at this thought but I did not mention it to my companions. We hurriedly went near Ma and did pranams. She then touched my friend Kajal and asked, "You all are Bengalees, is it not?" Kajal replied, "Yes, Ma, we were Bengalees. Are you also a Bengalee?" "Why", Ma said, "Do I not look like a Bengalee? I have of course heard many people remark that I am not a Bengalee." My other friend, Bina, remarked: "Really, Ma, you do not now look like a Bengalee." We all then left Ma and proceeded towards the main temple to offer puja. While we were a little away from Mother, we heard from behind Ma's ripples of laughter and these words: "Many people doubt that I am not a Bengalee. Ma Jagadamba knows who I am. Misled you are, misled you are. None of you could recognize me."

We then entered the sanctuary of the temple and offered puja. Anxious as we all were to go back to Ma, we hurried out there and ran for that side of the verandah where we had found Ma sitting. But we were disappointed to find the place empty. We then went round the temple in search of Ma and her party, but they could not be traced anywhere.

Disappointed, we went to the priest of the other temple to renew our request to offer us an idol of Gopal. Surprisingly, the priest readily agreed and offered us an idol which was just like the idol in size and appearance which my friend's mother had seen in the dream.

Mother's Birthday celebrations that year were to be performed in Bombay and Ma arrived in Bombay in time for the celebrations. I was bubbling with excitement to ascertain whether Ma was physically present on that particular day at Amba Devi Temple. One day getting an opportunity to talk to Ma in private, I asked Her about it. With an air of disbelief and utter innocence, She put a counter

question: "Were you all then day-dreaming or did
you go that day to the temple after taking something special?" But I insisted on receiving a direct
reply. Ma then asked me to call in Didi and when
Didi came, Ma told her smiling, "Didi, just listen
what she says. She tells me that she along with
three others saw Anandamayi Ma at Amba Devi's
Temple on that day." On hearing the incident, Didi
asked me to relate it to others.

Out of Mother's infinite karuna (compassion) and
to remove my doubt, Ma said, "When four of you
saw me, then it might be possible." Getting Ma's
confirmation, my heart overflowed with joy at the
thought that although She was on that day physically
present at Dehradun, she appeared before us for a
while at Amba Devi's temple in Bombay out of her
limitless compassion for her children. Jai Ma.*

Words of Ma

**What this body always says is: "Become a
pilgrim on the path of Immortality. Shun
the road that leads to death: tread the path
of Immortality. Bring to light that you are
imperishable, immortal.**

*   *   *

**You have not seen HIM, but you are yearning
for Him — because He is your very own. Does
one pine for that which is seeing? One's own
has been lost, or rather is hidden behind a
screen, and this is why one is hankering after
it.**

* As narrated by Smt. Arti Lodi

Chapter 8

MOTHER'S INFINITE KARUNA*

The incident related below took place about 22 years ago in the month of March. The exact date on which it occurred has been forgotten but the incident itself is ever green in the memory of the person who has had the great good fortune of witnessing it.

Mother was at Banaras. She had been entreated to visit a large school and in her usual kind way had consented to go. Mother and her then very small party arrived at the institution in the cool of the evening. Through a lovely garden lit with coloured electric bulbs, she was taken to a beautifully decorated rostrum. We all sat down around her, and then some people began to sing *kirtan*.

Abhoy and myself were sitting right at Mother's feet. Abhoy carried a small roll containing Mother's bedding, while I held her slippers in my hand. Suddenly when the *kirtan* was in full swing, Mother got up from the dais. I at once put the slippers down and she thrust her feet into them. Then she walked swiftly out of the pandal, Abhoy and myself following her. Mother sped away like the wind, and we actually had to run to keep pace with her. The garden was very large and the entrance quite a

Karuna — compassion

distance way, but we found ourselves at the gate in a few seconds. Just then a gentleman was alighting from his car. He had evidently come for Ma's *darsan*. He seemed astonished to see her walk away with only two companions. He folded his hands and asked what we were doing at the gate. Mother appeared to be in a great hurry. She at once requested him to take her to the railway station. He hesitatingly opened the door of the car and Ma got in at once, asking us to get in 'quickly, quickly.' The door was shut behind us and the gentleman drove us to Banaras Cantt Station. As soon as we arrived there, he asked Mother where she wished to go. "To Sarnath", was the reply. The gentleman explained that there was no train to Sarnath until the next morning, but Mother insisted. So he went to purchase three first-class tickets to Sarnath while we sat in the waiting-room. He had hardly returned with the tickets when a train steamed into the station. Mother stepped into an empty first-class compartment and we followed, while the gentleman kept on murmuring that this was a Mail Train which would not stop at Sarnath. Mother, however, paid no attention to his remonstrances, and soon the train left the station.

Within a few minutes it stopped (as happens at times when there is no 'all clear' signal). Mother opened the door of the compartment and got down. To us she said, "Come down, come down quickly." Abhoy jumped down with Mother's bedding-roll in his hand, but I was rather afraid to follow suit as it was impenetrably dark and I could hardly see anything. Moreover, being rather bulky, such athletic

feats as jumping down from a train were beyond
me. While I was still hesitating, Mother stretched
out her hand. The train whistled and in desperation
I risked the leap. It was not a moment too soon, for
the train steamed off immediately. We then found
that we had alighted near Sarnath station and that
we were standing between the railway tracks.
Mother asked us whether we knew the way to the
then newly-built Birla Dharmasala. Neither Abhoy
nor I had ever been there before.

Mother then started walking and we followed
her. We were plunged into complete darkness, with
no light showing anywhere. We had no idea where
Ma was leading us. Eventually, after covering quite
a distance, we came to a large gate. The doorkeeper
told us that this was the entrance to Birla Dharama-
sala. Mother went in and we after her. It was quite
dark inside the Dharmasala also, but Mother
advanced unhesitatingly in a certain direction. She
seemed to know exactly where she wanted to go.
She passed along a large verandah and pushing
open a door, entered a room. A small lantern was
burning there. The room was quite empty except
for a couple of wooden couches placed against the
walls. Mother walked straight to one of those and
in an indescribable tone of voice compounded of
laughter, tenderness and all the compassion in the
world, she exclaimed, "Here I am, here I am." We
now noticed the figure of a woman who sat up
sobbing loudly. Mother put her arms about her,
repeating "Here I am, here I have come . . . . don't
cry anymore." We went closer and recognized in
the weeping woman a certain Maharattan who was

an old devotee of Ma. She gradually gained control over her desparate crying and we all proceeded to the roof of the building and sat there for some time. Soon Ma's party arrived from Banaras. The gentleman who had brought us to the station had reported to Didi where Ma had gone and then conveyed her and the others to Sarnath.

Mother was in wonderful spirits, laughing, talking and joking with Maharattan. We had a very late dinner and then all went to sleep on the roof near Mataji.

It transpired later that Maharattan had come from some far off place to see Ma. On reaching Banaras, she had been told wrongly that Ma was at Sarnath. Without enquiring further, she had hired a tonga and proceeded to Sarnath, only to find that Ma was not there, nor was she even expected there. In the meanwhile, the tonga had left and there was no train to take her to Banaras. So she was stranded for the night all alone in a huge, empty dharmasala. To make matters worse, she was running a temperature and feeling quite ill. When she had been crying desperately for Mataji, Karunamayi Ma suddenly appeared in her room. This is only one of the innumerable examples of Mother's loving kindness and mercy. Jai Ma.*

Words of Ma

To cry out to Him is never in vain. So long as no response is received, the prayer must be continued. It is but the Self that calls to Itself, and none other than the Self

*As narrated by Sidhu

that realizes Itself. By ceaselessness in prayer, He who is whole (akhanda) is found. One's own Self (Atma), the Life of one's life, the Beloved of one's heart is the one to be eagerly sought. How many times have you not come into the world, craving and experiencing its fleeting joys and sorrows. The prayer, the invocation of Him, by which the opposites of renunciation and enjoyment are blotted out, this invocation has to become most dear.

*   *   *

Action directed towards God alone is action — all else is worthless, non-action, activity on the path of death. To become absorbed in Svakriya, the action that ends in Self-revelation is man's duty as human being.

*   *   *

Only you exist, you and you alone. Truly, you are contained in everything. Again, you are indeed THAT Itself. In all infinity is HE and no other — I alone am.

*   *   *

Man appears to be the embodiment of want. Want is what he thinks about and want indeed is what he obtains. Contemplate your true being — or else there will be want, wrong action, helplessness, distress and death.

Chapter 9

MOTHER — A SAINT OF THE HIGHEST ORDER

On the eve of the summer vacation of 1925, my very revered friend Rai Bahadur Pran Gopal Mukherjee, the Dy. Post Master General at Dacca, invited me there, holding but as a bait the likelihood of hearing the exposition of the Bhagavata by two very learned Goswamis and also meeting a "Maji" who, the Rai Bahadur added, had impressed him very deeply. I did not give much thought to the "Maji", but accepted my friend's invitation with some alacrity as both the Goswamis he mentioned commanded great respect as sound exponents of the doctrine of the Bengali School of Vaisnavism. So I went to Dacca; and a day or two after reaching there, I accompanied the Rai Bahadur and Srijut Nani Gopal Banerji, then Lecturer in Sanskrit, Dacca University, to Shahbag, a magnificent garden of the Nawab of Dacca. The late Ramani Mohan Chakravarti, known subsequently as Bholanath, husband of Ma Anandamayi, was then Superintendent of the Shahbag gardens.

Ramani Babu was then living in a small building in the garden with his family, i.e., Ma Anandamayi and one or two other members. There were two rooms in the building, one rather small and the other a little bigger. The shades of evening were gathering, and the extensive and carefully tended garden looked sombre owing to the tall and leafy trees, filling our hearts with reverence, while the sweet perfume of the numerous flowering plants near by added a rare charm. We were given *asanas* (small-sized carpets for sitting on the floor) in the bigger room and near the door between the rooms, sat Ramani Babu while in the small room sat Mataji. She did not yet speak to any stranger, and questions put to her would be answered through Ramani Babu. She sat partly veiled so that I could not get a full view of her face.

No sooner had I taken my seat than I felt myself in a peculiar state of mind, of which I had had no previous experience and the reason for which is yet a mystery to me. I had gone to see Mataji with hardly any preconceived notion, and indeed I did not expect to be very much interested. The state of mind of which I speak is difficult to describe; in any case I cannot give an adequate idea of it. All thoughts and ideas seemed to have vanished from my mind; and practically oblivious as I was of the surroundings, there was a sense of pleasure, very great pleasure, arising from what I do not know. Almost as long as I was in the presence of Mataji, my mind was in that state. I left the place, however, with the Rai Bahadur, somewhat surprised at what had happened, and spoke to him about it on the way. He gave me the sastric name for it. What struck me then, as it strikes me now, is that this was an experience which came, as it were, of itself. I should have regarded it as accidental, were it not for the fact that a similar experience came to me

next year (1926) at 'Shibnivas' in the Nadia district
in the same circumstances, i.e. sitting near Mataji
while the evening closed upon us. I was therefore
led to think that on both these occasions, Mataji,
for reasons best known to her, induced the peculiar
state of mind in me, and since I found it very
pleasurable, I felt attracted towards her. Thus began
an acquaintance which her ineffable grace has
ripened into a relation no whit less dear than the
dearest in the world.

By 1927, Mataji began to talk to all who sought
her blessings, without the restrictions she had impos-
ed on herself so far. Oh! For the glorious days we
passed in her company then! Now she does not
enter the dwelling-rooms in the residence of grihas-
thas (married families); and wherever she goes, she
has to be accommodated in a temple dharmasala
or ashrams. But in those days, she came to our
homes just like a member of the family. The ladies
of the house would prepare their beds alongside
that of Mataji where they would sleep with her. But
generally sleep there would be very little, for there
would be kirtana and conversations with her till
very late at night, sometimes even till the early
hours of the morning. On those occasions, Mataji
would listen sympathetically to all, sometimes speak
of her own early experiences and above all, by
kindliness of speech, gracious looks and sweet
manners, inspire not only love and affection for her
but also a faith that her presence enveloped us and
would protect us in all circumstances. We did not
care to ask ourselves whether she was a Siddha
Mahatma or an Avatara (Divine Incarnation). We

felt that she was Mother and that we might depend upon her. Could we but be with her always in this life and hereafter, we thought we would be perfectly happy, and more we did not want. Thus it is seen that she made an assault upon our hearts, and they were hers before we knew it — the intellect came into play much later.

In February 1945, Mataji's bhaktas (devotees) at Berhampore (Bengal) made arrangements for celebrations lasting for a fortnight in view of her presence in their midst, and some sannyasis and sadhus travelled all the way from Benares and other distant places to attend the function. I met there a very learned Swami of the Sri Sampradaya who had come from Vrindaban. In the course of conversation, he asked me: "What do you think of Anandamayi Ma?" I replied in a noncommittal manner: "The Divine Power (Daivi Sakti) seems to be manifest in her." The Swamiji said: "Mataji is certainly a saint of the highest order. We cannot however, believing as we do in the Sastras (Hindu Scriptures), agree with people who declare that she is an Avatara or that she is the Bhagavati herself."

Another very old saintly person, widely recognized as a sadhu of high order, on the other hand, prostrated himself before Mataji, saying "that was the Universal Mother Herself (Svayam Jagadamba)." When someone asked Mataji why she allowed him to fall at her feet, for at this his disciples were mortified, she replied: "Tell them that the feet of the Baba are always on my head"

I am of the opinion that for us it is an idle and

entirely meaningless discussion whether Mataji is an Avatara or Siddha Mahatma. While all other creatures come to the world in accordance with the law of Karma, the Avataras come of their own free will. Siddha Mahatmas, as is well known, are also free from maya and come to the earth of their own free will, proceeding from their samskaras of doing good to the world. Some hold, however, that the difficulty of regarding Mataji as a Siddha Mahatma is unsurmountable. For we have no information of any sadhana by her in this body.

On this point there is no room for any doubt. I have made enquiries for myself. The first occasion when Mataji was discovered to be in Bhava Samadhi was when she lived in our village (Astagram), and I have the evidence of reliable people, indeed of everybody living near about the place, that it lasted for nineteen hours during which she was, as it were, lifeless, so much so that ants gathered round her eyes. The different stages that she seemed to pass through after this, came naturally and were completed within a short time and also without any instruction whatsoever from any living being, indeed, for some time, in spite of the opposition of relatives. All this points to the strange but incontrovertible fact that the various stages and forms of sadhana or spiritual exercises and evolution took place automatically in her body without any active agency on her part. The theory that her siddhi has not been attained in this body but in a previous one, does not either seem to be tenable since she has said that she had no previous birth.

Again, "Brahmavid Brahma eva bhavati" (one who knows the Brhaman becomes the Brahman Himself). This too, some hold, is not applicable to Mataji because, as she says, there has never been any question of knowing or not knowing so far as she is concerned. This superconsciousness may be regarded as her very nature (svabhava). This diversity of opinion regarding her essential nature, hardly touches Mataji and her reply to those who ask her: "What really are you?', hits in my opinion the nail right on the head. She says: "I am what you think I am."

In 1927, when Mataji was staying with us for a day or two at Rajshahi, the late Professor Aswini Kumar Mukherji put some questions to her. In those days, Mataji used to have Bhava Samadhi, sometimes so deep that she seemed almost lifeless. Hardly could any respiration be perceived and the pulse felt at the wrists. Sometimes, again, she would roll from one end of the room to the other; and on one particular occasion in 1926, I remember she moved forward and backward on a fairly large platform in the Asram of the late Balananda Brahmachariji Maharaj at Deoghar. Her movements were so rhythmical and yet so awe-inspiring that I, for one, was reminded of the Cosmic Dance of Devi Kali. Again at times, Mataji would in her avesha (trance-like state) utter sweet and sonorous stotras (verses) not however in ordinary Sanskrit and with a preponderance of seed mantras (bijas).

Referring to Mataji's deep samadhi, Professor Mukherji asked: "How do you feel when you are in that state?" I am afraid she will not answer such a question now. She tried then also to avoid answering; but the Professor, old as he was, respectfully insisted. Mataji then said: "As you sit in this room, you can see everything outside through the doors and windows, but when they are shut you cannot. This body feels as if all its doors and windows were shut. Again when you take a handful of mud and wash it in the water of a pond, you see how finely it spreads on the water. So does this body feel." I do not know what Prof. Mukherji understood, but to me the meaning was clear. I understood Mataji to say that she became inwardly conscious while her outward consciousness received a check for the time being and she had a sense of expansion — Infinite Consciousness and Infinite Expansion.

Then the Professor asked: "Do you perceive the presence of any God or Goddess at that time?" Mataji tried to parry a good long while, saying that gods and goddesses might be seen if one wished to do so. But the Professor insisted: "Do *you* see them?" And finally she said: "They were seen before." I understood, therefore, that she had passed from all forms to the Formless. Thus must all seekers after Truth and Reality do before their efforts are crowned with success. (In Mataji's case, there was never any effort. All the various stages came to her of themselves and as a play, not in order to attain anything.)

Mataji, to me, is one through whom shines forth in all its effulgence the Infinite, and when I bow down to her, I bow down to it (Tat). At the same time, however, I am not blind, nay I value very much the human kindness in her, her solicitude for the least of our comforts when we are with her, the sweetness of her speech and smile, the affectionate inquiry about our welfare. Call her an Avatara if you like or a Siddha Mahatma if you prefer, it makes no difference to me for all practical purposes.

Is it a tiny tot that has been brought to her? See how her face beams. Does a school or college girl want to talk to her? How kindly she receives her! Can you be half as tender as she is to the sick and decrepit? And has anybody ever had elsewhere such a balm of sympathy at the loss of a near and dear one? Yet, if you are tired of walking in the mazes of philosophy, in a few words she points out the way and you are thrilled with surprise and delight. Or if in your sadhana, a knot has to be straightened out, seek her help and see what happens. Avatara, Siddha Mahatma, whatever she may be above all she is the Mother, ever tender, ever helpful, radiating love and affection. Her very sight purifies and ennobles.

That expression "shines forth", which I have used, reminds me of an experience. It was in 1926 or 27 at Shahbag and I saw her on my way to my native village. It was about 9 o'clock in the morning. She was sitting on a cot in a small room and I was squatting on the floor. There was some ordinary conversation and for a fraction of a second, I looked away from her. The next moment when I turned to her, gone was the Bengali lady and instead a resplendent form with light shining out of every pore of her body dazzled my eyes. I remember, I asked myself: "Where is the third eye?" On other occasions as well, I noticed similar transfigurations. It seems

to me, she no longer has these transfigurations, nor
does she have avesh or samadhi. Instead she seems
now to live forever on a plane difficult or impossible
for ordinary people to conceive. Once she was asked
in my presence whether those who are ever conscious of the Brahman, have dealings with people.
Her reply was in the affirmative. I feel she is now
like that. Sympathetic and tender she undoubtedly
is, yet a mystery seems to envelop her. I feel she
has travelled away from us although I know that
nothing can be more false than this. She once said:
"Are we separate?" Nay, Ma, I know we are not
and in this knowledge is bliss; but I want to realize
the truth of it, be always conscious of it.

Were I to point out one characteristic which
above all shines in Mataji, I would at once say,
"Non-attachment." She is kind, no one can be
kinder; she is affectionate, no one can have more
affection; she is sympathetic, no one can be more;
she is solicitous of our welfare, I have not seen
greater solicitude in anyone. My young daughter-
in-law was with her at Vindhyachal for a few days
and every letter she wrote was full of the description
of what Mataji did for her, how she took care of her.
So that in spite of her shyness, she was not in the
least uncomfortable. Even now, when speaking of
Mataji, her face lights up with joy. This is the feeling
everyone has in the company of Mataji. And yet
she is completely non-attached, nay it is because
she is unattached that she can be so affectionate,
so sympathetic, so kind. A non-attached person
having no axe of his own to grind is the fittest to be
really charitable and kind. From this non-attach-

ment again proceeds another peculiarity of Mataji: nobody, whatever his character, seems to be un- welcome to her. Her patience too is inexhaustible. In Calcutta, I have seen her surrounded by innumer- able people almost the whole day and far into the night. She had the same gracious demeanour throughout and her kindly smile never left her face. People of all sorts and conditions come to her and probably no one goes away without feeling, however slightly, the better for the visit.

The next characteristic of Mataji that I would mention is her unwillingness to impose her will upon anybody. I have never known her do so. She suggests, she recommends, she says it would be proper to do such and such things under the circum- stances, but with a fine delicacy of feeling; never insists upon anyone to follow a particular line of action, both in matters earthly and spiritual. Indeed, the liberty she gives to all, often makes us apprehend that there is not sufficient cohesion among her followers. This however does not trouble her in the least, for she is not out to form any new sect or party. On the contrary, all sects and creeds dissolve of themselves in her presence and under her influence.

Mataji is absolutely without any sankalpa, i.e. motive. This sounds strange to ordinary mortals, to all those persons who let actions proceed from a purpose. When asked what should be done in future regarding anything, her habitual reply is "Jo ho jaye" — wait for whatever happens. This is not putting off things in the manner of lazy men and women, but it means that she acts spontaneously on the inspiration of the moment. Frequently has it happened during her travels that railway tickets have been bought at her direction for places not very far, although her ultimate destination was far enough. Starting from Calcutta, for instance, tickets were purchased for Banaras, where again without interruption, the journey was continued to Delhi and then in a similar manner to Simla. This kind of motivelessness I have noticed in other great saints as well. It is this want of purpose that makes Mataji's actions tantamount to Lila and, indeed, the actions of personalities like her make it possible for us to believe that the whole universe is the Lila of the Eternal.

Mataji's way of bringing others to her point of view, if necessary, is also peculiar. I will give an instance. It is well-known that Bholanath would, at times, like a stubborn child insist on doing things that happened to come to his mind. In this, as in many other things, he was a veritable child, simple, frank, truthful and always anxious to help. Mataji, as is also well-known, would never directly go against his wishes. Indeed on this point, as in everything else, she set an example to the most devoted of wives. On a certain occasion in my house at Rajshahi, Bholanath insisted that a goat should be sacrificed. I was in great difficulty, for I could never think of doing such a thing. As luck would have it, someone happened to bring a goat along to the great joy of Bholanath. I spoke to Mataji, without his knowledge of course. She said, "Wait and see what happens." I was extremely worried. She, in the meantime, lay down and seemed to go to sleep. Preparations were made to take the goat with suitable puja to a Kali temple. There was some delay; in any case arrangements for the sacrifice were not made quickly enough, and when the party with the puja materials arrived at the temple, the priest said that Dasami (tenth day of the moon) having set in just a few minutes before, there could be no animal sacrifice that day. I did not think I was yet out of the woods, for Bholanath might have insisted on the sacrifice the next day, but to my great relief he forgot all about it. And Mataji? What did she do? She sat up when the party had started for the temple.

Neither by knowledge of the Sastras nor by sadhana am I qualified to say what Mataji really is. To me, she is more or less a fascinating mystery, an attractive and elevating personality with Infinity brooding over her. To know her is definitely blissful. Thousands all over India and abroad have now come in contact with her and have been attached to her. It is not at all likely that all of them will have the same idea about her. May we have regard for all of them nevertheless for truth is elusive and have many facets. Dull uniformity is not its hall-mark. The man who sincerely regards Mataji as but a woman of extraordinary spiritual development is in my opinion more blessed than one who lightly talks of her as a divinity that has strayed into our world of dust and storm. The great thing is to fix our attention upon Mataji, her words and actions, not at all the sundry theories and legends that float upon the stream of popular opinion. I may even go further and say that we should beware of the legends.

May the bliss of Mataji descend upon us all! May we all realize the truth about her! May we all be one in her Infinitude. Jai Ma.*

Words of Ma

This body does not advise you to renounce your home and repair to the forest. Wherever you may go, as long as you are not free from desire, there will be your home with all that it entails. No matter where you may be placed, you should meditate there itself, engage in sadhana. Just as when drops of water keep on falling, even stone is pierced, so by sustained practice the veil of ignorance will finally be rent.

For the aspirant who, is a householder, his wife is an embodiment of the divine sakti, his son of Balgopal. While leading a family life, do your work as the manager of the Lord. When the call comes for you to leave, none can accompany you. Of course, it has happened many times that husband and wife, who dearly love one another, get drowned together. But this is the fruit of delusion and not a desirable death. They are suicidals. One should drown for God. The human body is meant to be dedicated to God, to be employed in the service of Him. The householder has to mould his life after the model of the ancient Rishis who had wives and

* As narrated by Sri G. Bhattacharya

children equally worthy, and lived as prescribed in the Sastras. And one who has taken
Sannyasa must observe the rules and regula-
tions of the Sannyasa Ashram. God is my
very self, the breath of my life, He is not
distant but exceedingly near. Wherever you
are and in whatever condition, there itself
begin to practise sadhana. Hold on with
tenacity to Him who will liberate you from
all worldly ties. You need not ababdon anyone, only cling to God with all your strength.
The bonds of family life caused by delusion,
(moha) are not to be fostered. With detach-
ment, rising above delusion, live a life of
service.

Chapter 10

SOME MEMORABLE ANSWERS

Question: Why do we fail to remember God's name?

Mataji: Since you forget to remember God's name, you do not find Him. Don't forget that whatever happens in this world, happens according to His Will. Everything is indeed God's. While in the waking state, sustain the constant remembrance of Him. Do good works. Pray! One should practise the repetition of God's name, prayer and austerities. At night before falling asleep, think over everything good and bad you have done during the day. With a prayerful attitude of mind, dedicate all your actions at the lotus feet of the Lord. With a devout heart overflowing with a sense of dedication, pray to God to bless you. Do not think: 'It does not matter if I do anything blameworthy; I shall ask God to forgive me.' On the contrary, you should endeavour to engage only in the most commendable deeds. You must never give a thought to any bad or reprehensible work. Pray and surrender yourself totally at the lotus feet of God.

Question: How can one sustain the remembrance of God throughout day and night?

Mataji: By practice. By constant practice, anything, howsoever difficult, can be accomplished. Those who meditate, whether their minds are able to concentrate or not, continue their meditation. Whether you like to do japa or not, try to adhere to the practice of it all the same. Make an effort to let your kind be filled with God's name at all times. Be it at home or anywhere else, remember that nothing exists outside God. The idea of duality is itself sorrow. Feel that you are an instrument in God's hand. To do what God makes one do is certainly the best. Verily God alone is the Manager of the whole world.

Question: We can neither free ourselves from our worldly ties nor do we love God; so, what will be our lot?

Mataji: If one were to come out of the jungle, one must clear it. Start clearing from where you are. By lighting a small fire, the jungle will be burnt up. By coming to the Guru, everything is achieved. If the disciple is patient and alert, everything becomes possible.

Question: Again and again doubt assails the mind. Is this a good sign or a bad one?

Mataji: It is natural that doubts should arise to those who are on the path leading to God. Until you reach the state in which doubts are impossible, they are bound to come. When problems arise, they also call for a solution. In the course of one's practice doubt will awaken. For those who have not started learning yet and those who have completed their course successfully, there are no disturbing doubts and questions. When queries arise and doubts divide your mind, put them before your Guru again and again. Whatever your Guru says, accept and follow without asking why or how. At the same time, proceed also with your spiritual practices. Just as you eat, drink, sleep, and discharge your professional duties regularly, so must you pray to God with the same regularity to make you free from doubts. By sustained efforts, fire will be lit and its heat felt as well. Once the fire of real knowledge is kindled, everything will be burnt to ashes. By giving a little, one receives a little; obtaining a fragment is worth nothing. When you pray for any particular thing, it will be granted to you, but you will not get the whole. Burn up everything in the fire of Knowledge or else melt everything through intense devotion.

Question: Mataji, every day I listen to your words and I also pay attention to what you say. How much have I heard you speak about God! And yet, when I get engrossed in my work, why do I not remember Him?

Mataji: Fickleness is one of the characteristics of the mind. For life after life, you have formed the habit of letting the mind turn outward. The mind is so used to it that now you will have to reverse its movement and make it turn inwards. So long as the mind's movement does not turn within, it is impossible to find God. Therefore try your utmost to make your mind face inwards. By becoming inward-turned, God, who is enthroned on the lotus of your heart, will be revealed. If the mind roams about outside, it is turned away from Him. By practising sadhana consistently, one attains a spiritual condition when all worldly conversations seem distasteful. One is unable to enjoy it. So long, therefore, as you do not enter the current that drives you inwards, you must continue your efforts to make the mind face within. The mind cannot simultaneously move in two directions. Aiming at the two is detrimental; try to realize the ONE. Worship God, but not for the sake of showing off. Become steady in your practice. What will be the result of this? You will continue to practise without let or hindrance. Later, you will transcend both practice and non-practice and realize oneness.

Question: God is all-prevading. How can this be proved?

Mataji: A teacher or professor tests his pupils. Why? The tests are meant for the benefit of the students, not of the examiner; the teacher ascertains how much his pupils have learnt. The purpose of examinations is to make the students realize their shortcomings. Before putting God to the test, you must first scrutinize yourself; you have to adhere to your practices, and it is God who is the Examiner. The examiner is beyond examination. The test is taken for your sake, so that you may know yourself. Many people do, in fact, practise sadhana with God-realization as their only end in view, but they do not pay attention to their shortcomings, such as anger and egotism, cupidity and greed. This is why they become diverted from their aim. Thus tests and trials are not for the professor but for the students.

Questions: Man's life is conditioned by his *prarabdha karma,* Where does free will come in?

Mataji: You must use your free will to find the Supreme. The practice (kriya) by which you advance towards Him (Purushottama) is precisely what we call Purushakara (free will or the power to decide for oneself). By God's grace, even your destiny may be modified. If a devotee's faith that his *prarabdha karma* can be changed by God's grace is firm, then this may become possible. There certainly are laws that regulate God's creation, yet nothing is impossible for Him. If you think that God's grace is also within destiny, this is so for you. If, on the other hand, you are convinced that God is more powerful than destiny, then HE may do anything for you. He provides for the worldly as well as spiritual needs of His devotees.

Question: How can the ordinary person acquire faith in the existene of God?

Mataji: By seeking the company of saints and of seekers after Truth, by listening to religious teachings, reading Scriptures and carrying out the injunctions of the Lord. Are you not the offspring of the Immortal? The Immortal is Self-effulgent and lets Himself be contacted through the company of saints. Any kind of work that one does is based on faith. By associating with pilgrims on the path to God, the fire of faith will be kindled into a bright flame. Children study with the faith that, like everyone else, they will also pass their examinations. In like manner, by watching other seekers, devotees or yogis, one gains the faith that enables one to tread that path. In reality, you are Supreme Knowledge, Supreme Bliss. In order to discover your true nature, it is necessary to remove the veil of ignorance; and for the purpose of removing the veil, one has to resort to the Path, to spiritual exercises, and so forth. By following with perseverence the method pointed out by the Guru, one finally discovers God; one comes to understand that all are His images and that actually there is no 'you' or 'I'.

Question: If God is the fountain of goodness, why should there be so much fighting, cruelty and sin?

Mataji: He is goodness as well as evil. He is everything. He Himself stages a play with Himself. He does whatever is necessary for the completion of His play.

Question: In this atomic age, the world with all the creatures will be destroyed by war. Is it possible to save it by spiritual means?

Mataji: Whatever is to happen, will happen. Why worry about it? He who does everything will do the needful. You are also one of His manifestations and are able to concern yourself with this kind of thing. But how much can you *effect by your concern?*

Question: What evidence is there to prove that the impossible can become possible?

Mataji: If the impossible were not possible, how could this question arise? Everything is indeed possible. From the worldly point of view, one distinguishes between the possible and the impossible. Sometimes you definitely decide to accomplish some particular work, yet by the play of maya (illusion), it is made impossible. But where Isvara (the Lord of the Universe) is concerned, this is not so.

Question: Is it not possible to go beyond desire and experience?

Mataji: If everything is possible, why should not this be possible as well?

Question: Is there any shortcut to this goal?

Mataji: By the grace of God, such a shortcut may sometimes be found.

Question: What actually do you call faith?

Mataji: When breathing and doubt cease, real faith is born. There are two kinds of faith, namely, blind faith and real faith. Real faith, which is, aroused by the touch of an Omniscient Being, does not depend on anything. One who has awakened to Pure Consciousness makes you conscious. But blind faith, the faith of the mind, is unripe and can be shattered. All the same, real and genuine faith quite often develops gradually out of blind faith. To illustrate my point: A certain sadhu had a disciple who was a thief. He would tell lies, since this suited his convenience, and refused to obey his Guru who bade him speak the truth. One day the Guru asked him to follow his counsel in blind faith for a certain number of days at least and be completely truthful in everything said and done. The disciple agreed. One night he broke into the Raja's palace and on being caught spoke the exact truth. The Raja was so much impressed by his frankness that he not only let him off, but also provided for him and his family, so that he was able to give up both stealing and telling lies. In this way, he gained real faith in truthfulness.

Question: Suppose an atheist lives an ethical and righteous life. Is he on a lower level than a faithful devotee?

Mataji: An ethical life purifies the mind. Even though one may have no faith in God, if one believes in some Superior Power or pursues a high ideal, this also will serve one's purpose. By living an ethical life, one progresses towards the realization of the Divine. If one believes in supermen, can it be said that one does not believe in God? To believe in God under a particular name is also a way.

Question: In this age of science, why is it difficult to believe in God?

Mataji: By studying science, the thirst for knowledge is aroused, and thus one awakens to the search after Truth. But the truth that denies God and all deities is a partial and one-sided point of view — it isn't a comprehensive vision at all. An integral, complete vision unites the point of view of science with that of faith. In a full vision, the standpoints of the believer and of the non-believer meet. To lay stress on righteousness and ethics will educate your character and eventually lead to perfection. A complete, unobstructed vision will open out. By accepting your own line wholly and with all its implications, you will finally realize all lines of approach.

Question: Having accepted something as an axiom, why should one allow questions to arise?

Mataji: So long as one has not attained to direct knowledge, questions are bound to crop up. As long as you dwell in the realm of the mind, there will be questions. Here one has to reckon with time and death. But time and death are of the mind, of that which can be taught and learnt. Beyond the mind, there is neither space nor time or death. On attaining to final equilibrium, the axiom will become an irrefutable truth.

Question: Some people are ot the opinion that visions, etc. that come through spiritual practices are due to an unbalanced mind. Is this true?

Mataji: An unbalanced mind is the cause of vision? How lovely God is manifest everywhere and you have to attain to the vision of Him. How can this vision be due to an unsound mind? To go beyond the pairs of opposites is the characteristic of enlightenment. How can this be achieved by a deranged mind? The vision of God cures even insanity.

Question: When little ants fall into water, we pick them out. Won't God have compassion on us and lift us up?

Mataji: There are two ways in which God bestows His grace — through a flavour and also through a disfavour. There is both good and bad in the world. Whatever path is right and proper for anyone, that God will choose. In the shape of disease, of *kriya,* of work, in every shape God's grace can be perceived. At the end of sorrow, it comes to light. There is yet another way of looking at it — by sending adversity, God destroys adversity. By making you ill, He purifies you. God alone is the true doctor who purifies you within and without. Now look at it from yet another angle. Who hits whom? Who is ill? That you see sickness is an error. Only God is present everywhere. HE and HE and none but HE.

Question: If a householder devotee is in trouble, is it right for him to pray to God for redress?

Mataji: Various attitudes may be adopted. There are those who have dedicated themselves entirely to God. They say: "My Lord, whatever you may do, howsoever you may keep me, it is all right, for they will be done." According to the state of people's minds, their conditions differ. Some are at a stage at which they just cannot help praying. Others, when visited by trials and tribulations feel disappointed with God and drop their religious practices. On the other hand, there are persons who turn to God more eagerly when in sorrow. And some remember Him with greater fervour when they are happy. In all circumstances, He is the great healer. Therefore, many are moved to appeal to Him in trouble. Then, again, a state is reached when one does not any more feel inclined to pray to Him for relief in adversity, pain, ill-luck, and so forth. To invoke God is always good. For whatever reason you may pray, with whatever motive — at least start praying to Him! Be it for alleviation of distress or for enlightenment, be it even for wealth and possession. The wise ever live in the remembrance of God.

Question: How can the mind be made content? By what method can the operations and processes of the mind be controlled and the Self seen face to face?

Mataji: By aspiring to self-realization, to the knowledge of one's own Self - the Atma. It is necessary to proceed along some definite line of Sadhana: be it by regarding oneself as the eternal servant of the Lord or as His child or by adoring Him as one's Beloved, be it by adopting the method of inquiry into the nature of the Self or any other path. Whatever be your approach, it is right for you. The sages of ancient times pointed out the way. A stage will come where all paths converge. The method indicated by one's Guru is the one to be chosen; at the end every path becomes straight and simple. On reaching Goal, one will realize that there are innumerable ways leading to it. To accord with the different inner qualifications of the aspirants, there is a variety of paths or modes of spiritual practice. To find God means to find one's Self, to know the Atma, then one awakens to the knowledge that the ONE is the sole Reality underlying the World. The mind can be made content only when one's real treasure, the Atma, is found

Question: How can the restlessness of the mind be conquered?

Mataji: By intense love for God.

Question: We do not want unhappiness and yet it comes. We want real and lasting happiness and it does not come. Why?

Mataji: Your desire for true happiness is not intense enough. Take the help of a Guru.

Question: What is the greatest sin and the greatest virtue?

Mataji: Forgetfulness of God is the greatest sin; His constant remembrance is the greatest virtue.

Question: Is it right to pray to God for all kinds of things?

Mataji: The most excellent prayer is for God Himself.

Chapter 11

LILAMAYEE MA

Given below are two miracle-laden incidents as narrated by my wife Smt. Tushar Chaudhuri who had the rare good fortune and privilege of travelling with Ma throughout the length and breadth of the country. The incidents reveal Ma's supernatural glory as well as Her unbounded affection and blissful compassion.

—Author

When I met Shree Shree Ma Anandamayee for the third time at Simla Kalibari, I was then a college student. Before this, I had the good fortune to have Mother's *darshan* on two occasions in Delhi. After this third meeting with Ma, my acquaintance with and reverence for Her grew deeper and deeper solely due to Ma's unbounded Kripa (blessings) and unaccountable compassion. Even now when I think of Mother's most intimate and often partial favour bestowed on a most ordinary and insignificant person like me, my heart fills with profound wonder. But who can comprehend Mother's Lila ? Many miraculous and unbelievable incidents concerning me had happened at Ma's Kheyal (spontaneous wishes) and all those now seem to be illusory visions of dreamland. Presented below are two of those miracle-laden incidents.

I

It was the month of April. Ma came to Simla from Solan where she stayed for a couple of days in the estate of Raja Saheb of Solan who was popularly known as 'Jogibhai' (this name was given to him by Ma). At Simla, Ma stayed with Her party at Kalibari (guest-house attached to Kali temple). Ma's arrival created a stir and roused keen interest in the local people, particularly the Bengali community which was very much anxious to have Ma's *darshan* and satsang. But my interest was not as keen as theirs mainly because I had till then no close contact with Ma although I had two earlier *darshans* of Her.

On Ma's arrival at Simla, my parents used to go daily for Her *darshan* and I used to stay back at home for my studies. One day, they insisted on my accompanying them and I agreed. On my doing pranam, Ma rewarded me with a fascinating smile which, surprisingly enough, generated a deep inclination in my heart to go to Her daily. Ma however seldom spoke to me for which I felt depressed but in spite of my mental depression, I kept on going.

At Kalibari, I used to hear many interesting conversations among the devotees about Ma's supernatural powers and miracles. Some devotees would describe Ma as Antarjamini (knower of everything that passes in other's heart), others remarked that at a single glance at one's face, Ma could at once know the uppermost thought in the devotee's mind, while some others said that Ma had appeared to different persons at different places in

different forms, such as, Ma Durga, Ma Kali etc.
But I was not impressed by such anecdotes which
sounded to me as nothing but fairy-tales.

It is a fact of life that at times there are situ-
ations when our mind and intellect refuse to accept
blindly whatever we hear, no matter how astonishing and uncommon the subject-matter might be.
I myself was a victim of such a situation as I could
not take for granted all that I heard about Ma's
supernatural powers and divine glories. I, therefore, took a challenging decision to test Ma as to
whether She actually possessed an uncanny power
of knowing exactly about the wishes and desires
that arose in a devotee's heart.

I knew that Ma was a great lover of songs and
during each darshan time Ma used to ask somebody from among the assembled devotees to sing.
Sometimes She would ask two or three persons to
sing. I therefore devised a plan for testing Ma. I
decided to go henceforth for Ma's *darshan* with a
strong desire in my mind to sing before Her only if
Ma asked me to sing. I did not divulge this decision
either to my parents or anybody else. I then started
to practice a particular song thoroughly at home.
My acquaintance with Ma at that time was only
superficial and it seemed not possible for Her to
know whether I could sing or not. As I did not
put much credence in those miracle-laden stories
which I heard from the devotees, I was bubbling
with joy in my heart at the thought that I would
surely win in the test planned by me.

For the next two days, I did not go to Kalibari
for Ma's *darshan*. On the third afternoon, I volun-
teered to go for Ma's *darshan* and my mother

accompanied me to Kalibari. When we reached there, we found Ma sitting on a cot in the big hall and radiating a transcendental Light all around. The hall was almost packed to capacity. Inwardly, my thought centred round the fact that my role that day was that of a mute tester and as such I intentionally took a back seat at quite a distance from Ma. Everybody in the hall sat absorbed and spellbound in Divine peace blissfully emanating from Ma. After some time, Ma answered to some questions put to Her by two devotees. Ma then asked one girl to sing and when she finished, She asked another. On my part, I entertained the hope that Ma would surely ask me to sing and defeat me in the test, thereby providing an unmistakable proof that Ma did possess an all-knowing and all-pervading consciousness. An hour ticked by and during this period, Ma did not even cast a single glance towards me. This indifference led me to conclude that I was going to win the test and Ma to lose. I fixed my gaze on Ma and decided that on coming out of the Hall after the *darshan* was over, I would boldly tell those who spin stories about Ma's supernatural powers that I had got clear proof that Ma did not possess such powers.

After a while, some devotees with the intention of leaving the hall, approached Ma to do obeisance. On seeing this, my own mother told me that it was time for us also to leave. I agreed. I went near Ma, did my pranam and as I raised my head to get up Ma said "Are you leaving now? Won't you let me hear your song? Just sing at least one song for me." I was stunned and dumbfounded to hear Ma's words. In reply I murmured: "My father is about

to return home from office. I have come with my
mother and the keys of the house are with us." Ma
replied "Don't worry. To-day your father will be
late to return home. First sing a song and then go
home."

I therefore sat down and as I was getting ready,
Ma said with a smile : "Sing that very song which
you have practiced so hard." At this, my astonishment knew no bounds and I wondered how Ma
knew all about my plan.

After I finished singing, I looked up and found
Ma looking straight towards me with a bewitching
smile on Her face. The smile seemed to communi-
cate the message that I have lost the contest and Ma
has won. My heart filled with joy. I felt a wonderful delight which was hitherto unknown to me. I
also realised that this was one of thousands of
mysterious incidents that very often take place
around Ma.

I then went to Ma and did pranam. Ma touched
my head with Her hand and smiled. I then left the
hall with the firm conviction that Ma is an all-
pervading Divine consciousness for whom there is
no limitation of space and time and that She is
undoubtedly Antarjamini, Jai Ma.

II

More than three months had passed after the
above mentioned incident. We were then in Delhi
and as Ma did not visit Delhi for a long time, I had
an intense longing for Ma's *darshan*. One night, I
had a dream about Ma's presence in Delhi. Waking
up in the morning I decided to get information

regarding whereabouts of Ma. In Delhi, She at that time used to stay in the compound of Dr. J.K. Sen's house at Hanuman Road. My problem was to find a person whom I could send to Dr. Sen's house. I did not like to bother my parents about this and as such I was inwardly restless. Strangely enough, after a short while sound of a bicycle-bell was heard from outside and in came Gopalu, son of Shri Manoj Chatterjee (a devotee of Ma). He gave the information of Ma's arrival last night at Dr. Sen's house and also conveyed Didi's (Guru-priya Devi) message for me to meet Ma. I was thrilled to the core, not only at the unexpected prospect of meeting Ma but also to find my last night's dream come true.

I hurried to Dr. Sen's house and met Ma. My heart was filled with joy to have Ma's *darshan* and conversation with Her. Next day Ma said: "To-morrow early morning I shall move to Vrindaban. Do you want to accompany me?" I replied : "Ma, I will be very happy to go with you but I do not know whether my parents will agree or not." Ma said : "Have a word with your parents and if they agree, then reach here in time." Dr. Sen told me : "Ma with Her party will start very early in the morning and as such you will have to come and stay overnight at this house to be sure to ac-company Ma." My heart sank as I sensed that it was well-nigh impossible firstly to make my parents agree to permit me to go with Ma to Vrindaban and secondly to allow me to pass the night at Dr. Sen's house. It was a double-edged problem for me to find a solution.

At home, I very humbly placed before my

parents Ma's proposal to take me to Vrindaban
for a few days. They flared up and bluntly said:
"No, we can't agree. You have not, uptil now,
stayed outside without us. How can you go alone
to Vrindaban?" I argued : "I shall go with Ma and
stay with Ma and so the question of aloneness does
not arise. Moreover, Vrindaban is not very far
away from Delhi and my stay there will be for a
few days only." But my pleading and argument
failed to soften their attitude and on my part, I had
no other alternative but to resort to pressure
tactics, such as, fasting, sobbing etc. This, however,
helped to melt the ice. My parents gave me permission but on condition that my old Seja Dadu
(my father's uncle), aged about 75 years, would also
go with me so that he could bring me back to Delhi
after two or three days' stay at Vrindaban. I accepted the condition and I was inwardly happy at the
thought of going with Ma and staying at least for
two or three days under Her Divine presence.

We were to start for Vrindaban at dawn of next
day. So, we got ourselves ready to pass the
previous night at Dr. Sen's house. On reaching
there at about 10 P.M., I narrated to Ma how I
obtained my parents' permission and that my old
and aged Dadu had been deputed to accompany
me in order to curtail my stay at Vrindaban. Ma
simply said : "All right." She then gave instruction
to somebody to make arrangements for Dadu's
night-rest. Dadu retired for the night. Lying down
in another room, I could not have a wink of sleep
mainly because of Dadu. How nice it would have
been, I thought if I could go alone with Ma to
Vrindaban and in that case, I could easily stay with

Ma for a longer period, but due to my bad luck, that was not to be...Suddenly, my wishful thinking was interrupted by the sound of urgent tapping at the door and then I heard somebody calling out my name. I got up in haste and as I opened the door, I was told that my Dadu was running high temperature and he was in delirious state. I was stunned to hear this most unwelcome news and felt very much dejected at the thought that Ma might be unwilling to take me with Her leaving behind my Dadu in that condition. I ran to Dadu's side and found him in stupor under high fever.

Being face to face with that sort of grim situation, I felt utterly helpless and being helpless I went to Ma for a solution. I informed Ma about Dadu's condition and implored : "Ma, what shall I do now? Shall I not be able to go with you?" Ma kept silent for a while and then replied : "In the circumstances, you will have to obtain permission from your parents to let you go alone with me to Vrindaban leaving behind your Dadu". I pondered over Ma's words for a few minutes and my heart sank at the suggestion of obtaining my parents' permission for the second time overruling their condition of taking Dadu with me. As about an hour only was left before the start of Ma and Her party, I hurriedly scribbled a note to my father informing him about Dadu's sudden illness as well as Ma's insistence for my parents' permission to let me go without Dadu. I sent the note to my father through a Gurubhai. Minutes ticked by and in that pre-dawn silence all around, I awaited the outcome of my appeal to my father with bated breath. I started praying to Ma to remove all obstacles and

difficulties and to make it possible for me to accompany Her to Vrindaban. After half an hour,
the Gurubhai returned and handed over to me the
same note that I sent. On unfolding the note, I
found at the bottom of it something written in my
father's handwriting. His reply was : "Permission
is hereby given for your stay at Vrindaban for two
or three days only. Will arrange to bring back
your Dadu in the morning." I ran to Ma and gave
Her the news of my father's permission. Ma heard
the news with beaming smile on Her face and a
twinkle in Her eyes.

How happy I was then to accompany Ma to
Vrindaban unencumbered of all obstacles which
Antarjamini Ma had removed in answer to my
fervent prayer. The mystery of Dadu's sudden
illness was, I realised, Lilamayee Ma's creation as
Her smile seemed to give the unmistakable hint.

Due to Ma's infinite grace and compassion my
stay with Ma was not for two or three days only as
my parents had originally sanctioned, but it turned
out to be an uninterrupted and blissful duration of
more than a month. From Vrindaban Ma first took
me to Haribabaji's ashram at Bundh (a village in
the district of Aligarh). From there we went to
Calcutta and from there Ma took me to Ardha
Kumbha Mela at Allahabad and from there to
Varanasi before I returned to Delhi. The memories
of those unforgetable days still linger in my mind
and I wonder how difficult it is for us to understand
where, on whom and in what way Ma may bestow
Her grace.   Jai Jai Ma.

Chapter 12

ABOUT THE ORGANISATION AND INSTITUTIONS THAT HAVE GROWN UP AROUND MA ANANDAMAYEE

SHREE SHREE ANANDAMAYEE SANGHA

The devotees of Shree Shree Anandamayee Ma felt the need to form an association to bring closer together the vast number of persons from all parts of India and abroad who during the course of years had come to Mataji again and again and had expressed a desire to be kept informed of Her movements, and of the activities around Her in which they wished to participate whenever possible. Mataji's Divine personality attracted more devotees, and in course of time a number of Ashrams sprang up in different parts of India. Activities and various functions also having multiplied, the need for establishing an organization to look after these was being felt all the more. The establishment and registration of SHREE SHREE ANANDAMAYEE SANGHA in February 1950, therefore, fulfilled this need and it took over the responsibility of looking after the problems relating to the ownership, management and activities of the Ashrams as well as to the co-ordination of their activities and functions.

Thus, with Mataji's blessings, the efforts of devotees were crowned with success and the Sangha took shape. It is important to note that Shree Shree Ma is in no way connected with the management or control of the Organization.

Aims & Objects :

The chief aims and objects of the Sangha may be briefly summed up as follows :

1. To endeavour "to carry the message of Mother and the glory of Her personality to the world," through organising functions and celebrations, issuing publications, and by other means considered suitable to deliver the nectar of Her words to humanity at large.

2. To manage, supervise and control all Ashrams, Temples and Institutions that have grown up around Mother and also to develop and organise new institutions.

3. To bring together in close contact the large number of devotees of Mother who hail from various parts of India and abroad and to promote and foster a feeling of brotherhood among them so that "by mutual co-operation, they may help themselves to spiritual enrichment and share the grace and blessings of Mother both individually and collectively"

4. To establish and maintain charitable institutions to serve the sick and the needy.

Management :

The entire management and control of the affairs, funds and properties of the Sangha vest in the Governing Body. The Executive Council works on behalf of the Governing Body, subject to its supervision and control.

Membership :

All persons irrespective of nationality, caste or creed, who have attained majority, are entitled to become members of the Sangha provided they make an application in writing in the prescribed form and agree to accept the objects of the Sangha and to abide by its rules

Ordinary Membership fee is Rs. 30.00 per annum and Life Membership fee is Rs. 1500.00 Sannyasis and Brahmacharis, desirous of becoming members, are enrolled gratis.

Finances :

The main sources of income of the entire organisation with all its Branch-centres, are voluntary contributions from generous devotees of Shree Shree Ma. Donations paid to the Sangha are exempted from Income-Tax under Section 88 of the Indian Income-Tax Act, 1961.

Accounts are regularly checked and audited by qualified auditors and published along with the Annual Reports.

Activities :

The following are some of the principal activities of the Sangha at present.

1. **Functions and Celebrations :** The most important functions celebrated by the Sangha, are Mother's Birthday and Samaym Saptah Mahavrata which lasts a week and during which the devotees undergo a course of spiritual discipline with restricted diet and regular practice of meditation, japa etc.

Other functions which are organised and celebrated are: Dussehra, Guru Purnima, Kali Puja, Annakoota. Sivaratri, Holi, Gita Jayanti etc.

2. **Publications:**

(a) A quarterly illustrated journal "Ananda Varta" is published in three separate languages- English, Bengali and Hindi. It contains articles regarding the philosophy underlying Mother's teachings or recording Her sayings and dealing with various aspects of Her life and personality besides giving information about Her movements. Contributions of general philosophical and religious interest are also included.

(b) **Books :** A number of books in English, Bengali Hindi and Gujarati have been published on the life and teachings of Mother.

3. **Ashrams :** The Sangha at present has about 25 Ashrams of its own in India and Bangladesh. A list of these Ashrams with their addresses is appended to this chapter.

4. **Educational Institutions :** Two educational institutions are run, viz., the Vidyapith at Almora for boys and the Kanyapith at Varanasi for girls. The main stress in these institutions is laid on inculcating moral and religious values and in imparting training according to the ancient Brahmacharya system as adapted to modern conditions. General education according to ordinary school curriculum is also imparted side by side.